Books are to be returned on or before
the last date below.

Web Metrics
for Library
and Information
Professionals

Web Metrics
for Library
and Information
Professionals

David Stuart

facet publishing

© David Stuart 2014
Published by Facet Publishing
7 Ridgmount Street, London WC1E 7AE
www.facetpublishing.co.uk

Facet Publishing is wholly owned by CILIP: the Chartered Institute of
Library and Information Professionals.

British Library Cataloguing in Publication Data
A catalogue record for this book is available from the British Library.

ISBN 978-1-85604-874-3

First published 2014

Text printed on FSC accredited material.

Typeset from author's files in 10/14 pt Palatino Linotype and URW Linear
by Facet Publishing Production.
Printed and made in Great Britain by CPI Group (UK) Ltd,
Croydon, CR0 4YY.

Contents

Introduction

Not everything that can be counted counts, and not everything that counts can be counted.

William Bruce Cameron (1957)

Increasingly it seems as though every organization, profession and service is subject to a mounting number of metrics and performance indicators. League tables are no longer reserved for the winning and losing of sports teams, but are used to make comparisons between a host of different bodies, from hospitals and schools to train companies and countries. The growth and interest in new metrics and indicators has been facilitated by the growth and interest in the web. The web facilitates the sharing of established metrics and data; a service such as Google Public Data (www.google.com/publicdata) now provides a user-friendly front end to a wide range of public data, enabling the simple comparison of countries according to features as diverse as the number of daily papers sold per person, to the contribution of renewable energy to a country's energy supply. The web enables the soliciting of new data; Web 2.0 services have facilitated the ranking of politicians according to their 'hotness' and professors according to their helpfulness. Most importantly, the web also provides new media for analysis; in the same way the traditional media of books and journals provided the basis for new metrics, such as the number of books published in a country or the number of citations a journal receives, so new media such as web pages and blogs provide the basis for a host of new metrics. These web metrics can be far richer than those associated with traditional media as a greater variety of data can be collected at increasingly fine levels of granularity.

This book demonstrates how a host of new web metrics can be an important addition to the library and information professional's skill set. Web metrics can enable librarians to improve the online service they provide to their stakeholders and demonstrate the impact of their services to managers and policy makers; web metrics can be used to help identify the most relevant resources in a field and demonstrate the value of their own online offerings. The library and information professional's online presence now comprises a wide variety of genres. Many libraries have Facebook and Twitter accounts, some host blogs and wikis, and a few make use of the newer social media services such as Pinterest or Google Plus. This book provides ways of establishing and analysing metrics, as well as highlighting the potential pitfalls. This first chapter provides an introduction to the topic and an overview of the rest of the book.

Throughout the rest of the book the term 'librarian' has been adopted as shorthand for the more longwinded 'library and information professional'. While the intended audience of this book includes many information and knowledge professionals who neither work in a traditional library nor consider themselves librarians, for the sake of readability it was necessary to adopt a more concise term. As has been seen in the recent discussions surrounding the rebranding of CILIP, the Chartered Institute of Library and Information Professionals, there is no single term with which the whole profession identifies, so the book has resorted to the most established.

Metrics

As 'metrics' form the basis of this book, it is important to start with a clear understanding of what is meant by a 'metric'. The term 'metric' is used throughout this book to refer to a *quantifiable standard of measurement*, or as the Oxford English Dictionary defines it: 'system or standard of measurement; a criterion or set of criteria stated in quantifiable terms' (OED, 2001). A quantifiable standard of measurement is one that can not only be reduced to an explicit number, but also be applied consistently in different situations to allow comparisons between similar objects of investigation.

Quantitative measurements form the basis of some of man's earliest records: the scratching of tallies on bones used to record work done and the possession of cattle in preliterate societies (Yeo, 2010). In such instances the standards that the scratches were based on were likely to have been fairly simple. For example, when the farmer marked off his number of cattle most people were likely to know what was meant by a head of cattle without the need to create a definition that explicitly excluded the field mouse. However, as society becomes more complex and trade is extended over greater distances, it becomes necessary for standards to become more explicit. Greater specialization means the same norms can no longer be assumed, especially between different communities. The extreme of such a situation may be seen in France in the late 18th century, where up to a quarter of a million different weights and measures were used throughout the country (Russell, 2005). Such diverse weights and measures have obvious implications for the free flow of trade, and the same is true with a lack of standardization in web metrics. If one company wants to place advertisements on another company's website, but there is no standardized way of measuring the number of page views of a website, a complex series of negotiations may need to take place. Equally, if a large multinational organization wants to engage the services of a social media marketing company, but there is no standardized measure of impact, it is difficult to determine whether the marketing company has met its objectives or it is being paid without delivering. It is therefore in people's interests to develop widely adopted standards, and they are beginning to emerge online.

Standards can emerge via consensus, imposed by an authority, or through a combination of the two (Russell, 2005). Where a diverse range of standards is perceived to have a significant impact on the economy or on the safety of individuals, standardization may be imposed by government, although in many areas standardization is left for a consensus to emerge from the community of interested parties. This is something that can be particularly difficult in a fast changing environment with new technologies disrupting existing systems. Such technological disruptions have become a well established part of librarians' work.

The community of librarians has a long history of engaging with metrics. Its own field of bibliometrics was defined by Alan Pritchard in the 1960s as 'the application of mathematics and statistical methods to books and other methods of communication' (1969, 349). Its roots may be traced back much further. While the application of bibliometrics was popularized by Garfield and Price in the 1950s, Godin (2006) traces the origins of bibliometrics to psychologists in the early 20th century, and Shapiro (1992) pushes its beginnings to the legal bibliometrics of the 19th century. Broadus (1987) goes even further, pointing to the forerunner of bibliometrics as being the simple counting of books or similar items that can be traced to the third century BC and the identification of 490,000 scrolls in the Library of Alexandria. However, even with a history dating back over 2000 years, answering bibliometric questions is not an easy matter, whether it is the number of items a library holds, or even the more specific number of books a library holds.

The question 'How many books does a library hold?' quickly raises issues regarding what is meant by a book and, in an age of e-books, what it means for a library to hold it. While we all have a vague idea of what is meant by a book that is sufficient for most everyday interactions, standardization requires an explicit definition, but there is no single universal agreed definition of 'a book'. UNESCO (1985) defines a book, for the purposes of collecting statistics on the production and distribution of printed publications, as 'a non-periodic publication of at least 49 pages exclusive of the cover pages, published in the country and made available to the public', but the US Postal Service (2012) defines a book as anything over 24 pages, with no mention of its availability to the public. Selecting one definition over another could increase or decrease the size of a library's holdings at the stroke of a pen. While it would be easy to be cynical about the public official who decided to select the less restrictive standard of what constitutes a book, and thus increase the size of the library at no additional expense, it is also easy to envisage situations where the stricter definition is inappropriate. For example, in a children's library where a large number of what most of us would consider 'books' have less than 49 pages, the US Postal Service definition of a book would seem a more appropriate definition than categorizing what many of us would consider books as UNESCO 'pamphlets'.

An even greater challenge to determining the number of books a library holds has been the introduction of electronic books in recent years. As libraries increasingly sign up to electronic publications, a focus on printed publications alone is obviously only part of the picture, but how should e-books be included if we are to be able to compare the holdings of two institutions? Is the subscription to a 10,000 e-book bundle more significant than the subscription to 1000 individually picked titles? Does a hyperlink to Project Gutenberg (www.gutenberg.org) from a library's website allow the library to claim an additional 39,000 e-books? What if the Project Gutenberg collection is incorporated into the library catalogue and librarians have used their expert knowledge to provide added value? If an e-book can be accessed by multiple users simultaneously does that count as multiple copies? There are no simple answers, although standards are being established for traditional and new media. COUNTER (www.projectcounter.org) is an international initiative to establish standards for exchanging usage information between publishers and libraries about journals, databases and book subscriptions, while the Web Analytics Association (a precursor to the Digital Analytics Association, www.digitalanalyticsassociation.org) has published definitions of a wide variety of concepts, such as 'page view' and 'referral' to facilitate communication and best practice in the analysis of web usage.

Although standards and definitions may have been created, that does not mean that the most appropriate metrics have been identified for a particular situation. There are numerous ways web content can be measured. In his marketing blog David Berkowitz (2009) lists 100 ways to measure social media. He includes many of the direct metrics that may be immediately obvious, such as friends (Facebook), followers (Twitter) and page views (blogs), and less obvious and direct metrics, such as the number of customers assisted and job applications received.

The appropriate metric depends primarily on the purpose of the metric, but where a comparison is being made between individuals or organizations the selection of a particular metric is inevitably contentious as the metric may be seen to favour one group over another.

Indicators

Metrics are not counted for their own sake, but for a purpose. For example, when a library counts its holdings and states that it has a collection of 1 million books it is generally expected to be taken as an indicator of the library's ability to support its users' needs. The use of such a metric as an indicator may be implied if the step is obvious or well established; for example, a library is unlikely to feel it is necessary to state that the size of the collection is an indicator of its ability to serve the needs of its users. However, when the use of a metric as an indicator of something wider is not obvious or widely agreed, its adoption can cause considerable animosity, especially when there are significant potential consequences.

Bibliometric methods established within the field of library and information science are regularly adopted within the wider academic community to provide indicators of individual and institution research excellence, although they have generally been met with a less than enthusiastic response by the subjects of such investigations. Following the announcement that bibliometrics would be contributing to the 2013 Research Excellence Framework (the way research quality is assessed in UK higher education institutions and which informs the way billions of pounds of funding is allocated) there was a raft of negative headlines regarding the use of bibliometrics: 'Metrics Will Kill Diversity Claim' (Lipsett, 2006); 'Popular Beat May Drown Out Genius' (Lawrence, 2007); 'Report: bibliometrics could distort research assessment' (Lipsett, 2007).

The concerns on the use of bibliometrics reflect those on the use of metrics more generally. There have been three main problems in bibliometrics being widely accepted for the provision of indicators of research excellence: a lack of agreement that research excellence can be quantified; concerns about the tools that are available; and concern regarding the impact of the indicators on the research and publication processes.

The sorts of concerns touched on above are not limited to the application of bibliometrics, but are equally relevant in the adoption of other metrics, especially when it comes to the letter of the metric over-riding the spirit of the indicator. For example, Banerjee and Duflo (2012) highlight a school in Calcutta that had a perfect pass record each year, but unfortunately this was achieved through a policy of expelling the bottom students in the class each year; the desire for a perfect pass rate surpassed the desire for the provision of a good education that the metric was designed to indicate. This does not mean that such indicators are useless, but rather that they need to be treated cautiously, especially in web metrics, where the creation of content is cheap and so much of the material is ephemeral.

Web metrics and Ranganathan's laws of library science

The term 'web metrics' is used throughout this book to refer to the quantitative measurement of the creation and use of web content. It would be hard to over-estimate the impact of the web on people's lives; it is not only a place that people go to discover information, but also one where they increasingly interact with one another and create their own content. Over the last two decades the web has transformed the publication of traditional forms of media, and introduced a host of new genres of digital media. The early home pages and websites have been joined by blogs and wikis and massive social network sites that have attracted millions of users. Twitter, Facebook, LinkedIn and Flickr are now essential platforms for many individuals and organizations, and those that ignore such platforms are potentially ignoring the opportunity to engage with vast numbers of actual or potential stakeholders. The type of content that is being published has also widened, from documents to data, from text to rich forms of media. All of these new media and platforms provide the opportunity for new ways for librarians to share information, and new metrics and indicators for librarians to measure this information. With so much that can be counted, it is important for librarians to keep in mind the underlying philosophy of library and information science and their role in the information ecosystem. Librarians who find themselves the holders of a particularly salacious piece of gossip about a celebrity may be in a position to increase their online impact rapidly, although it seems unlikely that such behaviour would adhere to the underlying philosophy of the library profession.

The goals of the library and information profession are not necessarily the same as those for other businesses, and the types of metrics that it needs to establish should reflect that. In his book *Social Media Metrics*, Jim Sterne (2010) emphasized the importance of identifying metrics that align with the three big goals of business: increase revenue, reduce costs and improve customer satisfaction. Each of these has its place in the library. The library needs to find ways to increase revenue and lower costs, but the key factor is customer satisfaction, and for that we need to consider the philosophy of library science as so eloquently expressed in Ranganathan's (1931) five laws of library science:

1 Books are for use.
2 Every reader his book.
3 Every book its reader.
4 Save the time of the reader.
5 The library is a growing organism.

These laws have been regularly reinterpreted to take into account new technologies and new types of content, whether new types of media (Simpson, 2008) or the underlying data (Stuart, 2011), and when identifying appropriate web metrics it is important to have these laws in mind. Web metrics can help us to determine whether books are being used, readers have access to the information that is needed, information is being pushed to those who need it, and we are saving the time of the reader, and to reflect the fact that the library is a growing organism.

Web metrics for the library and information professional

While Ranganathan helps us understand the goals that librarians should be striving for, there are many ways in which web metrics can be used to help reach those goals. Behn (2003) identified eight purposes for measuring performance by managers in public organizations: to evaluate, to control, to budget, to motivate, to promote, to celebrate, to learn and to improve. Each of these purposes could drive librarians to establish a web metric, with the same web metric potentially contributing to more than one purpose.

Evaluation is generally the usual reason for measuring performance, and it is for research evaluation that bibliometrics have so often been adopted (e.g., Moed, 2005). However, the evaluative value of web metrics is not necessarily as obvious as the value of bibliometric indicators. While the importance of visitors to an online storefront may be seen as central for some organizations, for others the relationship may seem less obvious. For example, a research group's success is not necessarily associated with its web presence to the same degree as it is with its research publications, yet some studies have nonetheless shown the number of links pointing to a website to be associated with an institution's research excellence and business sites' success (Vaughan and Yang, 2012). The number of Twitter followers or 'likes' of an organization's Facebook page may also be seen as the success of a brand on the social web.

To *control* is to ensure that people are behaving appropriately. While a library may use the metric of its number of Twitter followers to evaluate the impact of its service, it should also make sure that it is engaging with those followers in the best way. It may choose to establish upper and lower limits on the number of tweets it sends in a particular day or week to provide a consistent level of service.

To *budget* is to allocate resources appropriately. On the web there is a host of ways librarians may attempt to engage with users, while the time available to librarians is normally extremely limited. Metrics can help librarians determine the most effective web technology for their particular purpose; new online services may take time to become established, but unless there are signs of growth after six months it may be that the service is not appropriate.

To *motivate* is to encourage users to reach goals. The web offers a wealth of potential opportunities, but its scale can be daunting. When the press reports on celebrities with millions of Twitter followers, or a YouTube video going viral and being watched a billion times, a library's social media offerings may seem extremely insignificant. It is therefore important to motivate with specific attainable goals in mind, and make comparisons with similar organizations or similar attempts by the same institution. It may be that the aim of a library's blog is to have so many thousands of readers, or a more explicit indicator of engagement, such as the number of comments left.

To *promote* is to convince the public, or those higher up in the organization, that they are doing a good job. Library budgets are constantly under scrutiny, and librarians need to demonstrate their value, although caution may need to be observed when a public institution is making use of a new technology the value of which may not as yet be widely accepted. Establishing a successful online presence is not something that happens overnight; although a blog can be set up within a matter of minutes, it may take months or even years to establish a significant amount of interest. Even if a library has established a successful presence on an online service, there is no guarantee that this will be considered to be anything more than a waste of time.

To *celebrate* is to revel in the organizational achievements. When shared goals are reached it provides the opportunity for groups to bond around the achievement. This could be the library's 1000th Twitter follower, the 500th download of its podcast, or the millionth visitor to its website.

To *learn* is to understand the impact of the contributions that librarians are making. In a world with fast changing web technologies it is necessary to determine whether a particular technology is effective. It is only through measurement that problems can be raised and dealt with. Is an organization's Twitter account found to be more engaging when controlled by one user rather than another? Has the web redesign, which so enamoured the managing director, really made any difference to the number of visits to the website?

To *improve* is to strive towards the provision of better services. It is not enough to learn that certain content elicits a more favourable response; librarians need to use this information to improve the service the organization provides. If metrics show that a new design to the website has failed to work, then the organization needs to learn from the experience rather than carrying on regardless.

Behn's (2003) eight purposes for measuring performance are internally focused, helping an organization have a greater understanding about its own workings and achievements. Web metrics also provide the opportunity for librarians to apply metrics beyond the organization: to filter; to research.

To filter is to use web metrics to help with the problem of information overload. Information overload is not new; in fact the story of scientific progress is one that is regularly punctuated by new tools to overcome the problem of information overload. The establishing of scientific journals in the 17th century solved the problem of scientists having to share the same results multiple times with different colleagues. As the number of publications increased, so did the tools to help researchers manage them. In the 18th century peer review (Kronick, 1990) and dedicated abstract journals (Skolnik, 1979) were introduced, while computers enabled large-scale citation indexes and full text indexing in the 20th century. The web has enabled the publishing of billions of documents and this requires new methodologies to deal with the information explosion unless we are going to wade through the 'tomes of irresponsible nonsense', a phrase that Ziman (1969) applied long before the invention of the web. In the same way that the journal impact factor helped to identify core journals, and PageRank helped to rank pages on the web, new algorithms can be expected to help researchers filter the increasing variety of content that is available online.

To research is to apply the quantitative methodologies of web metrics for research purposes. As has been argued elsewhere (e.g., Stuart, 2011), while the work of librarians may continue to revolve around the provision of traditional document formats (books, journals and articles) for the foreseeable future, as traditional aspects of librarians' roles are automated and as the web changes from a web of documents to a web of data it is important that the role of librarians also changes. This means not only providing users with access to traditional types of document, but also facilitating user access to the huge quantities of data that are increasingly available online. Some libraries already provide a research service for bibliometric data, from citation analyses to mapping the researchers in a particular field. Web metrics can provide additional insights to such traditional bibliometric studies, and make it possible to gain insights into a wide range of research questions, such as public opinion on topics as diverse as genetically modified crops and the latest computer games release (Thelwall, 2009) to predicting the winner on celebrity reality shows (Tancer, 2009) and the spread of diseases (Eysenbach, 2006).

The aim of this book

The aim of this book is to demonstrate the contribution web metrics can make to the work of librarians.

The focus is primarily on those tools that are freely available, or at least have useful functionality that is freely available, even if there is more extensive functionality that may require a subscription. Most librarians are unlikely to have the budgets necessary to subscribe to the increasing number of firms that offer access to a wealth of web metrics at a price, but that does not mean they cannot gain insights from the tools that are freely available. There is currently little consensus about the appropriate standards and metrics to use for particular purposes for many of the different media that are discussed throughout the rest of the book, or hope of an authority imposing a widespread set of standards in the near future. Instead librarians are generally left to muddle their way through, reaching for the nearest metrics that are freely available, whether these are those most noticeable on the service that is being used (e.g., number of friends on Facebook or number of followers on Twitter) or one of the increasing number of third parties that promise a simple solution to a person's metric needs (e.g., Klout.com, Alexa.com). This book aims to introduce metrics to the community of librarians, and help them understand why one metric may be more useful than another, and the limitations of the tools that are available. New metrics will emerge and become accepted within the creative destruction of the marketplace, and this book is designed to reflect practices and ideas that have been put forward by academics and practitioners, applying standards and methodologies to new areas, with a focus resolutely on the contribution to librarians.

The book does not attempt to hide the limitations of web metrics or their antecedents, but rather sees their potential as semi-evaluative and weak-benchmarking metrics (Thelwall, 2004b). It is not that it is necessarily wrong for one website to have 1000 visitors a month, when a similar institution's website has a million, but it is something that warrants further investigation. Metrics should not be the end of a conversation, but rather the beginning. Not everything can be easily reduced to numbers, and it may be that one individual or institution does not do as well as another because their particular strengths are not reflected in the adopted metric. In such cases it is not unreasonable for a manager or governing body to ask why there has not been the expected impact, but it is important that there is room for an individual or institution to make a case for their particular circumstances.

The structure of the rest of this book
Bibliometrics, webometrics and web metrics (Chapter 2)

Chapter 2 looks more closely at the variety of metrics that have been adopted within the library community and how they relate to web metrics. Areas such as bibliometrics have an established history within the field and have faced many of the objections that may be levelled against web metrics. While recognizing these limitations, the chapter emphasizes the potential of a wide range of metrics to the community of library and information professionals, as well as the importance of measuring what is important to librarians, and the lessons that may be learnt from the traditional media environment and applied to the web.

Data collection tools (Chapter 3)

Web metrics are heavily reliant on the tools and data that are available, and

Chapter 3 considers how these tools have developed and changed over the past two decades in the area of webometrics. There have been four distinct periods of webometric research, as researchers have adjusted to the changing nature of the web and the tools available for investigating it. These periods provide insights into the limitations of web metrics that are caused by the structure of the web and those that are caused by the changing nature of the tools, and potential changes that may occur in the future.

Evaluating impact on the web (Chapter 4)

Despite the rise in third-party social media services, self-hosted content continues to be an important part of many libraries' web presence, as well as a potential source of information about other organizations and society more generally. Chapter 4 considers metrics for measuring the impact of websites, blogs and other hosted content, from the use of analytic services, to references on the web. It also discusses the use of content analysis to gather additional insights into this highly unstructured data source.

Evaluating social media impact (Chapter 5)

Third-party social media services have an increasingly important role in the hosting of content, providing opportunities for the establishment of new metrics and new problems for data collection. Chapter 5 considers the types of metrics that should be considered for different types of social network sites, and the potential adoption of sentiment analysis enabled by the ever more structured content.

Investigating relationships between actors (Chapter 6)

Web metrics are not restricted to evaluative purposes, but may also be used to provide relational insights on the web and the social web. Chapter 6 considers some of the tools and techniques that are available for mapping and analysing the relationships between online entities.

Exploring traditional publications in a new environment (Chapter 7)

As new genres of online media grow in importance, traditional bibliographic items continue to be the most significant part of most librarians' work, whether the traditional hard copy format on the shelves, or an electronic version thereof. However, new technologies provide new avenues for the investigation of the impact of traditional formats, whether mentioning texts online, or counting the number of document downloads or bookmarks in Mendeley's reference manager.

Web metrics and the web of data (Chapter 8)

The web is moving from a web of documents to an ever more semantic web. Not only are library repositories expected to host raw data as well as documents, but websites are increasingly marking up data within web pages. This requires the development of new metrics if we are to understand the data that is being made available and the impact that it is making. This chapter discusses some of the challenges that need to be overcome, and some potential solutions.

The future of web metrics and the library and information professional (Chapter 9)

The future is likely to bring the introduction of new technologies, increased pressure on library budgets, and a greater emphasis on the use of metrics. The final chapter discusses the challenges and issues this raises for librarians and offers some potential solutions so that librarians can meet future challenges with confidence.

2
Bibliometrics, webometrics and web metrics

Introduction

Web metrics for librarians combine tools and methodologies from the information science community with the goals and applications of the marketing community.

The first part of this chapter explores the relationship between web metrics and associated terms from the information science community (e.g., bibliometrics, scientometrics and webometrics), as well as its relationship with web analytics from the marketing community. Within these different areas web metric investigations may be broadly categorized as either relational or evaluative. The second part of the chapter looks more closely at the theoretical basis and practical investigations that can be considered under these headings, and how such investigations may be applied by librarians. The final part of the chapter considers the validation of web metric findings.

Web metrics

The term 'web metrics' is used throughout this book to refer to the quantitative measurement of the creation and use of web content. It has been adopted as a broad term, inclusive of the many different uses to which web metrics have been put and for which varying terminology has emerged over the years. In the style of Björneborn and Ingwersen's (2004) diagram of the metric terminology, Figure 2.1 (overleaf) shows the overlapping scope of the different metric terminology used within this book, with web metrics, the shaded area in the diagram, comprising web bibliometrics, web scientometrics, altmetrics, webometrics and web analytics. The sizes of the ellipses are not indicative of the size of the research areas, but rather are for the purpose of clarity. Each of the areas that form web metrics is discussed in more detail below.

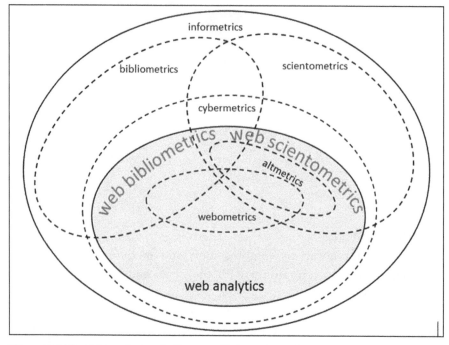

Figure 2.1 'Metric' terminology in library and information science

Information science metrics

Information science has coined a number of 'metric' neologisms over the years. Some have become widely adopted (e.g., bibliometrics), some have been short lived (e.g., internetometrics), and some remain extremely niche areas of investigation (e.g., discometrics). It is important to define the terminology clearly so researchers can be understood by one another and science policy makers (Lazarev, 1996). It is through the overlapping of the associated metric terms that we can understand how the different areas contribute to web metrics and the potential of web metrics to contribute to a librarian's professional activities. The different metric terms coined by the information science community are broadly of two types: those that relate to the items being measured, and those that relate to the purpose of measuring the items. There is a lot of overlap between the two.

Informetrics

Informetrics give the broadest measure of content, the study of the quantitative aspects of information in any form (Tague-Sutcliffe, 1992). As information may be considered the basic property of the universe (Stonier, 1999) there is plenty of scope for informetric investigations, although its use is generally restricted to the quantitative study of communications between people. Most informetric investigations have focused on the sub-domain of bibliometrics.

The medium: from bibliometrics to webometrics

The term 'bibliometrics' was defined by Alan Pritchard as 'the application of mathematics and statistical methods to books and other methods of communication' (1969, 349). In most instances the particular methods of communication under investigation have been journals and books, primarily those of the academic community, and it is in this more restrictive sense that it is used within this book. It could be used more broadly to refer to any document, but analysis of other resources has often resulted in the coining of new terms for the particular resource type: the term 'patentometrics' has been used to refer to the application of bibliometric methodologies to patents (Mortensen, 2011); and 'discometrics' for the application of similar methodologies for scores and sound recordings (Rorick, 1987; Schubert, 2012). Bibliometrics may also be used in a more restrictive sense to refer to the analysis of the bibliographies within books and articles (e.g., White and McCain, 1989), although this is more restrictive than its general usage and would exclude a lot of literature for which there is not a more suitable term.

The rapid adoption of the web in the mid-1990s, as well as the recognition of the similarities between the linking between web pages and citations between journal articles, led a number of researchers to recognize the potential of the web and the internet as the basis of informetric investigations. Suggested names for this field of investigation included 'netometrics' (Bossy, 1995), 'internetometrics' (Almind and Ingwersen, 1996), 'webometrics' (Almind and Ingwersen, 1997) and 'cybermetrics' (Aguillo, 1997).

Of these the term 'webometrics' has become widely adopted within the information science community, initially conforming to Björneborn and Ingwersen's (2004, 1217) definition: '[the] study of the quantitative aspects of the construction and use of information resources, structures and technologies on the Web drawing on bibliometric and informetric approaches'. 'Cybermetrics' continues to be used, albeit to a lesser extent, to refer to the investigation of the internet more generally rather than just the web specifically. More recently, however, webometrics has gained a more specific definition. Thelwall (2009, 6) moves the meaning of webometrics away from the topic of quantitative aspects, and more towards the purpose: 'the study of web-based content with primarily quantitative methods for social science research goals using techniques that are not specific to one field of study'. These quantitative methods for research purposes are not restricted to the social sciences, but may equally be applied to other disciplines, and webometrics is used within this book to refer to the study of web content with quantitative methods for research purposes. It is therefore useful to distinguish between web metrics more generally, and webometrics in the narrow research sense, with the term web metrics used throughout this book to refer to the quantitative measurement of the creation and use of web content.

The shift in the meaning of webometrics to a specific purpose aligns it with other subgenres of informetrics, which revolve around the purpose of the metrics, such as 'scientometrics' and 'altmetrics'.

The purpose: from scientometrics to altmetrics

The beginning of scientometrics is generally traced to Price's (1963) seminal work *Little Science, Big Science,* where a quantitative approach was taken to understanding the structure of modern science. The term itself, or at least the Russian equivalent, was coined by Nalimov and Mulchenko in 1969 to refer to studies into 'all quantitative aspects of the science of science, communication in science, and science policy' (Hood and Wilson, 2001, 293). In practice, for many years, the majority of scientometric investigations generally consisted of bibliometric investigations, in addition to a smaller number of studies investigating the application of bibliometric methodologies to patents (Narin, 1994). The application of bibliometric methodologies to patents may be representative of increased recognition of the importance of interactions between science and industry to the innovation process (e.g., Lundvall, 1992; Gibbons et al., 1994; Etzkowitz and Leydesdorff, 1995). Even with the addition of patents, however, traditional scientific publications provide only a limited picture of scientific discourse, and more recently greater attention has been given to the establishing of alternative metrics.

The web has enabled a wide range of forms of communication outside the traditional forms of publication, and provides new ways of measuring impact within the academic community and for other sections of society. This measuring of impact is something that is particularly easy when information is structured in a standardized format, and the dominance of a small number of social network sites means that millions of users now have certain information structured in a similar fashion. The term 'altmetrics' was coined by Priem et al. (2010) to refer to making use of the structured nature of Web 2.0 technologies to establish alternative filters and indicators of research impact. Today the primary focus of altmetrics is with the impact of traditional scientific outputs online, although there is the potential for altmetrics to provide far wider insights into scholarly communication. Within this book a broader definition of altmetrics is considered, encompassing the impact of non-traditional forms of communication that may also form part of a researcher's output.

Web analytics

It is important to recognize that there are uses of web metrics that do not have their antecedents in the bibliometrics and informetrics of the library and information science community, most noticeably in the case of web analytics with its background in the realm of marketing. Marketing is not interested in the potential of web metrics to provide insights into some abstract theory or the growth of science, but rather in gaining insights that can contribute to the successful trading of products and services. The term 'web analytics' is used here to refer to the application of web metrics for understanding and optimizing web usage.

Some of the most innovative tools and technologies have been developed for the marketing community, even if in some cases the tools they produce may be used beyond the purpose of understanding and optimizing web usage. For example, Google Trends (www.google.com/trends), Alexa (www.alexa.com) and Majestic SEO (www.majesticseo.com) are examples of tools that were initially developed for marketing purposes and have since been used by the academic community for research purposes.

Although there is undoubtedly a place for web metric methodologies to be used by librarians for research purposes, there is also the more practical application of these tools for marketing purposes. For example, a librarian might be interested in the impact that their personal blog is making, or a library manager might want to determine whether they are engaging with their users in the most effective manner.

Relational and evaluative metrics

As has been shown above, web metrics have a wide range of uses, from the researcher investigating the growth of scientific domains to the individual wondering how many visitors their website has received. Rather than detailing every type of investigation that is possible within each of the areas identified, as well as their theoretical foundations, it is more useful to categorize the metrics broadly as either relational or evaluative.

In an analysis of bibliometrics for scholarly communication Borgman and Furner (2002) identified seven facets by which bibliometrics could be classified. Their analysis included the type of scholarly behaviour that is the focus of the investigation (linking, writing, submission or collaboration), the level of the aggregation (person, group, domain or country) and the goal (description, explanation, prediction or evaluation). Within this book web metrics may be broadly categorized according to the approach that is taken: relational or evaluative.

These broad categories are used within Borgman and Furner's (2002) bibliometric typology to add a finer level of granularity to the discussion of linking behaviour. Analysis of linking behaviour in the form of citation analysis has been the principle form of bibliometric analysis, although Borgman and Furner choose the term 'linking' rather than 'citing' as in an age of electronic versions of documents inter-document connections do not need to be restricted to citations. Relational link analyses investigate the relationships between actors, whether these are individuals, organizations, journals or articles. An example of a relational link analysis is a study of how researchers are connected via a co-citation analysis (authors are found to link to the same academic papers). Evaluative link analysis refers to studies that use links as indicators of the quality or impact of an actor, whether a journal, researcher or research group, most often through the use of citation analysis.

The terms 'relational analysis' and 'evaluative analysis' in this book are not restricted to their use in link analysis, but rather are used to distinguish between two distinct approaches to the investigation of any web metric entities: relational web metrics focus primarily on the relationships between entities; evaluative analysis is where a value is being inferred from an entity's relationship with other entities. In some instances the difference between relational and evaluative analysis is just one of perspective, with the same methodology forming the basis of both.

Evaluative web metrics

Evaluative metrics are generally considered the most important part of bibliometrics and web metrics. It is for generally measuring the impact of academic research that bibliometrics is most of interest, and tracking the impact of web content that web metrics are mostly used.

There are many different ways the web impact of particular entities may be measured, and many different entities that may have their impact measured. And while they may be of interest for web analytic purposes, evaluative web metrics are of interest for webometric, web bibliometric and web scientometric purposes as well. In each instance, however, we are referring to a web object and an associated measure of impact, analogous to the journal article and citation that have been the focus of so much bibliometric analysis. A diversion into the realm of evaluative bibliometrics helps demonstrate some of the potential, problems and limitations of web metrics.

Evaluative bibliometrics

Evaluative bibliometrics have for a long time been recognized as a set of tools to help librarians manage their collections. As libraries rarely have unlimited budgets, it is useful for librarians to have a way of identifying the core journals for their particular users. The journal impact factor was developed as a method to identify additional core journals for the Science Citation Index, and is calculated by dividing the number of citations in a year to articles published in the previous two years by the number of articles published in those two years (Garfield, 2006). The step from calculating the impact of journals to ranking journals is a small one, and the creation of the Science Citation Index in the 1960s simplified the process by which researchers could gain access to citation data, especially citations outside their own particular field, and the term 'impact factor' has now evolved to encompass both journal and author impact.

Increasingly bibliometrics are being used to assess the impact of individuals' and groups' research outputs: governments are interested in the potential of bibliometric indicators as they attempt to identify the best method of allocating research funds, while institutions are interested in bibliometrics as a method of tracking the impact of academic outputs. In the worst case scenario journal impact factors are used as a surrogate for a paper's impact, as they are easier to calculate and do not necessitate waiting for a paper to actually be cited. There is huge variation in the number of times papers within a particular journal are cited, with a few papers responsible for much of a journal's journal impact factor, and there are campaigns against the misuse of journal impact factors (e.g., San Francisco Declaration on Research Assessment). Even if more author-centric measurements are used, while reducing an author's research output to a single figure enables simple comparisons to be made between individuals, there is a host of different ways such a figure can be calculated. In his paper introducing the h-index Hirsch (2005) listed four: total number of papers, total number of citations, citations per paper, and number of significant papers (with significant defined as papers over a certain, arbitrary, number of citations). Each may be seen to have advantages and disadvantages: the number of papers published measures productivity, but it does not measure the impact of those papers; the number of citations measures impact, but may be inflated by a small number of highly cited papers; citations per paper may penalize high productivity, while the number of significant papers may randomly favour or penalize researchers according to the arbitrary level it is set at, with different levels appropriate at different stages of a researcher's career.

Hirsch's h-index was proposed to address the disadvantages of previous methods of evaluating a researcher's output with a researcher having an h-index of h if they have published h papers and each of those papers have been cited at least h times (Hirsch, 2005). For example, if author A has published five papers, and they have citation counts of 5, 4, 4, 2 and 1, author A will have an h-index of 3 as there are three papers that have been cited at least three times. The idea that a researcher's impact may be reduced to a single value is understandably appealing for evaluation purposes, and since its invention there have been a number of variations to address perceived limitations of the h-index. Bornmann, Mutz and Daniel (2008) identify eight:

- The m quotient is designed to address the problem of someone's h-index primarily reflecting the length of their research career by dividing the number by the number of years of research activity.
- The g-index is designed to increase the weight given to highly cited papers, with an author's g-index being the highest number g of papers which together receive more than g^2 citations.
- The $h(2)$-index is also designed to give more weight to highly cited papers, with a researcher's $h(2)$-index being the highest number of $h(2)$ of papers that have each been cited $[h(2)]^2$ times.
- The a-index is the average number of citations for the papers in the Hirsch core (those papers that are sufficiently cited to contribute towards a researcher's h-index).
- The m-index is the median number of citations for the papers in the Hirsch core to address the skewed nature of the distribution of citations.
- The r-index takes the square root of the number of citations in the Hirsch core. This is a reaction to the perception that the a-index punished researchers for having a higher h-index.

- The *ar*-index adapts the *r*-index to take into account the age of the articles in the Hirsch core.
- The h_w-index is an adaptation of the *h*-index that takes into consideration citation impact.

It is ironic that the appeal of reducing a researcher's output to a single number has spawned such a wide range of metrics, and there are few signs that there will be an agreement on a single most appropriate metric. Bornmann, Mutz and Daniel's (2008) paper suggests that part of the reason for this is that the *h*-index variants fall into two categories: one type measures the size of a scientist's productive core of research, and the other measures the impact of the productive core. Multiple metrics give a better indicator, and they recommend that any two complementary metrics are used, although if only one is to be used then one that measured the impact of the productive core could be a better predictor of peer assessments. However, if only one measure is used, there is little benefit in using one of the more complex variations of the *h*-index (Schreiber, Malesios and Psarakis, 2012).

Despite the appeal of reducing each researcher's work to a single value, such a measure inevitably over-simplifies the value of a researcher's work and there are risks in assigning too much credence to the metrics. This is something that is not denied by those developing the metrics. Garfield (2006) writes of the 'inherent dangers', although he also recognizes that most people do not have time to read all the relevant papers. Hirsch (2005) points out that 'a single number can never give more than a rough approximation to an individual's multifaceted profile, and many other factors should be considered in combination in evaluating an individual'. Nevertheless, the simplicity of the single metric has captured the scientific community's imagination, and when Google Scholar introduced their 'my citations' feature (http://scholar.google.co.uk/citations) they not only included the *h*-index, but also introduced one of their own that measured the number of significant papers, the *i10*-index, which is the number of publications that have received at least ten citations (see Chapter 7 for a fuller discussion on the use of metrics within Google Scholar). Both the citation report for a selected set of papers in Thomson Reuters' *Web of Knowledge* and the citations overview for a set of papers in *Scopus* also calculate the *h*-index for the particular set of papers.

There is a great diversity in the number of times a piece of research is cited. At one extreme is an article by Lowry et al. (1951) that has at the time of writing been cited 301,039 times, while at the other are the millions of articles that are never cited or cited only once or twice. This does not necessarily mean these were bad articles, or that they have not contributed to scientific discourse, but rather the value of some of these articles is not necessarily being reflected in citations, the established currency of academia. As MacRoberts and MacRoberts (1996) have pointed out, there are many concerns regarding the use of citations as an indicator of value: authors do not cite all the papers that have influenced their work; when all influences are not cited those that are included may be biased in favour of friends, colleagues and self-citations; secondary sources, such as review papers, may take preference over original research; and authors cite papers for many different reasons, including the refutation of the findings of the cited article. While a bibliometrician may argue that many of the problems even themselves out on average, the concern remains that good research could fail to be recognized while bad research is rewarded by the use of citation metrics. This is especially likely when looking at increasingly fine levels of granularity. For example, the impact of a country's or university's publications may even themselves out on average, but a small department or individual may adversely suffer (or alternatively excessively benefit) from any divergence from model citation behaviour towards their few publications. Whether or not such fears have any grounding, they nonetheless continue. In a study into how scientists perceived citations, Aksnes and Rip (2009) surveyed the views of Norwegian scientists who had published highly cited papers. They discovered that although the scientists considered citations to correlate with the contributions of their own work, they were highly cynical about citations more generally.

There are undoubtedly cases where citations are given to articles that are not necessarily of good quality. Following the Schön scandal, where a physicist fraudulently claimed a number of breakthroughs in the field of semiconductors, a number of leading journals retracted articles they had published. The seven articles that were withdrawn by *Nature* currently have 62, 29, 165, 132, 224, 171 and 136 citations respectively (according to Google Scholar); this is a cautionary tale for anyone assigning too much weight to the 'quality' of citations.

The biggest concern regarding bibliometrics for scientometric purposes should not be the current failure of the metrics to reflect the impact of research adequately, but the potential for a negative effect on the scientific process, especially as the metrics gain increasing importance. This may be seen as the information equivalent of Gresham's law, which is popularly stated as 'bad money drives out good money' (Rolnick and Weber, 1986). This is the idea that if good and bad money have the same face value (the bad money is over-valued) the bad money will drive the good money out of the system. Within bibliometric analysis certain features are given the same value, irrespective of whether they are of equal worth. For example, peer-reviewed articles may all be valued the same, or citations received counted equally worthy. This can lead to the situation where authors are driven to publish more than is necessary, or court controversy and exaggerate the implications of findings in an attempt to increase citations. This point is neatly summarized by another law of economics, Goodhart's law: 'When a measure becomes a target, it ceases to be a good measure' (Strathern, 1997, 308). Those who want to shun such practices, but rather adhere to the traditional norms of science, may feel that they have no choice but to adjust their working behaviour if they are not to be surpassed by those who, at least according to the metrics, have more successful research.

With citation analysis continuing to be a contentious issue for evaluative purposes, and the appeal of being able to reduce a researcher's work to a single metric, it would seem as though there is little room for web bibliometrics in evaluative scientometric investigations. After all, while citations may be placed for a variety of reasons, peer-reviewed research nonetheless has a level of credibility that is lacking from much of the content on the web. What is required, however, is not the reduction of research to a single metric that sums up the whole of a researcher's work, but a battery of metrics, which may be of varying robustness, that can nonetheless combine to provide a fuller picture of the research process. For this web metrics have a lot to offer.

Evaluative web bibliometrics and web scientometrics

The potential of web metrics for evaluative bibliometrics has been recognized for a number of years. It is over a decade since Harnad et al. (2003) suggested that the UK's Research Assessment Exercise (RAE), the precursor to the current Research Excellence Framework (REF), by which millions of pounds of research funding are distributed in the UK, could stipulate the use of online CVs for researchers with links to open access articles. This would enable a far wider range of scientometric indicators, including the number of downloads an article receives, to encourage the investigation of input beyond the corpus of documents represented within established citation databases.

The most immediate advantage of web metrics for evaluative purposes is speed; web metrics can potentially provide a faster indicator of the impact of a work than traditional citation databases (unless of course the journal impact factor is being used as a surrogate). The traditional publication process continues to be a drawn-out process. A work may be highly influential in the development of another piece of research, but the process leading to a citation can be long and arduous. First, the research that is influenced may need to be carried out. The paper must then be written, hopefully with the original paper still in mind. The paper must then go through the peer-review process, which may be a long drawn-out process, especially if the original submission is to a journal with a high impact factor. Finally the paper is published, although this may still be a long time off as there is likely to be a backlog of journal articles to fill the next half-a-dozen issues. By this time the original influential author may have already had an appraisal meeting, and been overlooked for promotion or moved on to new pastures. Web metrics offer the potential to give early indications, whether in the form of bookmarks or discussions in blogs and on Twitter or downloads of journal articles.

It is this potential for a wider variety of more timely metrics which has driven interest in the altmetrics, and there is an increasing number of tools available for measuring the impact of academic research on the web. The rise of Web 2.0 technologies, such as blogging platforms and social network sites, have provided anyone with minimal technological skills and an internet connection with their own publishing platform, and have increased the publishing of structured data. These include aggregating services that may require a subscription, e.g., Altmetric (altmetric.com), and those that are free, e. g., Impact Story (http://impactstory.org), in addition to which an increasing number of journals are not only sharing information about the number of times a papers is cited, but also alternative metrics. For example, PLOS ONE publishes views, citations and academic bookmarks.

Altmetrics provide a new means of ranking actors. For example, in December 2012 the journal *Nature* published a list of articles that had had the biggest impact on social media (Van Noorden, 2012). Such rankings do not have to follow traditional measures. For example, in its *Global Research Report* Mendeley, the academic social network and reference manager, enabled the ranking of institutions by the time researchers spent online and the number of papers in their online libraries (Mendeley, 2012). A number of studies have shown the correlation of altmetrics with the traditional indicator of scientific impact – citations. Bar-Ilan (2012) showed a correlation between the readership of articles on Mendeley and the number of citations papers received, while Eysenbach (2011) showed Twitter mentions to be an early indicator of citations. The real importance of altmetrics is not a replication of citations, but a different perspective on the impact of work, an alternative that is equally valid.

Online scientific communications are not restricted to electronic versions of traditional communication, but come in an ever increasing number of formats. Every new technology is seemingly tested for its suitability in aiding scientific discourse, and those new technologies that are adopted offer the potential for new metrics to provide new insights into academic discourse. Such metrics may provide insights into informal communication within or beyond the scientific community:

- Wikipedia edits could provide an indicator of a medical researcher's attempt to improve public health information.
- The number of views on a YouTube channel could be an indicator of a scientist's public engagement.
- Reputation achieved on a question and answer site such as Stack Overflow or similarly designed sites on the Stack Exchange Network (http://stackexchange.com) may indicate a high level of engagement with a research community.

Although the research article continues to provide a useful format for sharing many research findings, there are necessarily many compromises as research is reduced to an explicit narrative that can fit into 20 pages. Scientific research rarely follows the neat journey chronicled within most academic articles; the methodology or tool that is presented as obvious, may in fact only have been discovered after numerous other tools and methodologies were found to fail. Not all knowledge can be easily captured in words; 'we can know more than we can tell' as Polanyi (1966, 4) stated, and he coined the phrase 'tacit knowledge' to refer to that which cannot be stated. Large data sets that would run to millions of pages if printed have understandably traditionally remained with the researcher, while the complex computer programs that test this data may be rendered meaningless when reduced to text.

The web enables new approaches to research practice and dissemination, including more open approaches to science. Open source science follows the open source approach to the development of software, with many researchers coming together on projects that may not be funded otherwise. For example, The Synaptic Leap (www.thesynapticleap.org) brings together biomedical science researchers to investigate diseases such as malaria and schistosomiasis (Kepler et al., 2006). Open notebook science is a person-centric approach to opening up science, 'organising the scientific production based on the public disclosure of achievements and failures, and their related data and procedures, so that they are analysed and discussed openly to further advance science by solving and addressing specific problems' (Vera, 2009).

Open notebook science provides a way of sharing the sorts of findings and data that have not traditionally made it into journal publication, although the publishing industry itself has also been changing. Video-based journals have been established in an attempt to capture information that is lost in the translation to a text format (e.g., the *Journal of Visualized Experiments*; www.jove.com). Publishers and librarians are more and more interested in the concept of enhanced publications, with the core journal article being linked to associated resources. This may be computer code, data, models or post-publication metrics. It is also possible to move beyond the notion of a final, finished article completed by a single author, and it has been suggested that scientific research has much to gain from the type of collaboration and versioning control that is adopted by the programming community (Hrynaszkiewicz, 2013). Most important is the fact that new forms of output are increasingly being recognized as legitimate by the academic community and research funding agencies. The *Journal of Digital Humanities* (http://journalofdigitalhumanities.org) does not request submissions in the traditional manner, but rather identifies work that has already been published on the open web, while in January 2013 Piwowar noted that the US National Science Foundation is now asking for researchers to list their research 'products' rather than 'publications'.

If such innovative approaches to science are to be encouraged, then it is important that we get away from the limitations of one-dimensional indicators such as the *h*-index, and enable a battery of indicators to provide a fuller impression of a researcher's output. Web bibliometrics will inevitably be compared with bibliometrics, with questions being raised about the robustness of any metrics that are based on data that is potentially relatively easily manipulated. As has been seen with the dominance of Google, a whole industry can quickly emerge that helps organizations build their online impact by either fair means (so-called 'white hat' search engine optimization) or foul ('black hat' search engine optimization). Although questions are often raised about the trustworthiness of citations, as friends and colleagues cite one another excessively, there can be little doubt that web links (or some other indicator of impact) are more easily created. As users try to game the system, new techniques will also emerge for identifying anomalies and potential abuses. It may even be the case that librarians have a role to play in the internal auditing of any evaluative web metrics.

Evaluative web metrics are not purely for the appraisal of research quality; they can also be used to identify resources that are likely to be particularly useful. Although journal editors and publishers may balk at the way journal impact ranking tables are calculated, they can nonetheless provide a useful tool in helping researchers identify the core journals in a field, or the highly cited papers that they may need to be aware of. It is important for the future of science, however, that such tools are far more open.

Search is now an integral part of the way many people live their lives, with no question too mundane to be worthy of a Google. For most people the search engine is a black box, and little thought is given to how the results are ranked or the results they may never see because they are not at the top of the first page. When searching for research papers on a topic in Google Scholar (http://scholar.google.com) or Microsoft's Academic Search (http://academic.research.microsoft.com) the ranking systems often seem more transparent than within traditional search engines, with the number of citations having a significant impact on the ranking of a paper, but relevance and citations are different and underlying algorithms could potentially have an impact on the direction research is taking. Especially as academic search services follow the lead of services such as Amazon's 'customers who bought this item also bought...' and use their databases to start recommending academic papers to read.

Academic search engines and journal rankings are undoubtedly useful tools for helping researchers find the information they need, although it is important that researchers recognize the limitations of these tools. It is not necessary for librarians to take the route of some academics and reverse engineer Google Scholar to identify the factors that contribute to Google Scholar ranking (e.g., Beel and Gipp, 2009), but they should nonetheless recognize there are other tools and approaches that may give different perspectives on a research field, and to remember that none of the tools should be thought to include everything.

Evaluative webometrics

As well as providing information about the scientific research process, web metrics also have the potential to provide insights into the activities of society and human nature more widely, and it is for the use of web metrics for research purposes that the term 'webometrics' is used within this book. The breadth of insights that can be gained from users' online activity reflect the breadth of uses for which people now use the web. As has been demonstrated in Bill Tancer's book *Click* (2009), queries can not only predict the winner of celebrity talent shows, and reflect the fact that there is a peak in visits to diet websites after Thanksgiving, but search engines can also provide insights into people's innermost thoughts. People enter their hopes and fears into search engines, asking questions they may be reluctant to discuss with their closest friends and partners; through their online searches we can discover people's health fears, what they want to do, places they want to go, and how these change over time and in relation to big stories in the news. Tancer is general manager of global research at Hitwise, a company that collects data from internet service providers to provide paying customers with insights into users' online behaviour across the web. He has access to vast quantities of data that most librarians cannot afford to access. There are, however, many other tools that can be used to gain insights into user behaviour that have been explored by the academic community, who like librarians often need to find tools that are free at the point of use.

Over the past two decades the way people have used the web has changed, and so equally has the way people analyse the web. We have gone from an era of individually created websites where the majority of web users were consumers of content, to an era dominated by a few commercial websites with the vast majority of web users producing as well as consuming web content. Evaluative webometric research has gone from analysing web pages and counting web links, to analysing an increasingly diverse range of content and relationships. Nevertheless, we are still talking about the analysis of entities that may form the basis of evaluative or relational investigations.

Ingwersen's (1998) original web impact factor was calculated by summing the number of external inlinks (incoming hyperlinks from outside the aggregation) and self-links (hyperlinks within the aggregation) to an aggregation of web pages by the number of pages in the aggregation. The original web impact factor could vary extensively depending on the design of a website and decisions by a small number of external websites. For example, if the same website content was distributed over 100 pages rather than ten and it nevertheless received the same number of inlinks then the web impact factor could vary by a factor of ten. Alternatively, if an external website makes use of a content management system that repeats a link on every page of a website (e.g., the blogroll of recommended blogs on the sidebar of a blog), a single person's decision to include a link may result in thousands of inlinks. To diminish the impact of any individual's decisions there have been experiments with a wide variation of web impact factors: alternative document models have counted links not from individual pages, but directories or websites (Thelwall, 2002); and alternative denominators to number of pages in a site have included the number of full-time equivalent employees (Li et al., 2003). The suitability of a particular variant of a web impact factor as the basis for a particular indicator (e.g., an institution's research excellence) have generally been validated through a combination of correlation with existing data (e.g., an institution's RAE or REF rating) and a content analysis of the reasons links have been placed.

Today webometric analysis is no longer restricted to web pages, or impact to be related only to web links. Units of analysis include company names and phrases, with metrics based on their appearance online or how often they are searched for. It includes distinct units hosted on some of the major social network sites, from profiles to images, with metrics based around concepts such as friendship, followers and views. Nevertheless the principles remain as they did for early link analysis: links (or whatever other substitute for impact is being counted) should be created individually and independently by humans, and be of equivalent value, while if any inferences are to be drawn from an analysis appropriate steps should be taken to validate the findings, generally through correlation with existing data and a content analysis of the reasons for link placement (Thelwall, 2004a).

Evaluative web analytics

Web analytics is the application of web metrics for the evaluation and improvement of a service, and it is the principal reason most people, including librarians, come into contact with web metrics. It has much in common with evaluative webometrics, although there is a difference in focus and action. Web analytics is primarily focused on one particular entity, and the results of the investigation are designed to drive action rather than be an end in their own right.

Most people are uninterested in bibliometrics and webometrics for research purposes, but are interested in the number of visitors their website receives, followers they have on Twitter, or friends they have on Facebook. It may even be argued that some groups are excessively interested in such metrics. In research into the use of Facebook by a group of university students Bornoe and Barkhuus (2011) found that the average student had 841 Facebook friends, with the person with the fewest friends having 187 and the person with the most having 2939. These numbers are not only far higher than the average Facebook user who has 130 friends, but also far higher than the number of people with whom people can sustain stable social relationships, the so-called Dunbar number, which is commonly taken to be around 150 (Dunbar, 2011). It may be argued that at this point Facebook friendships have very little to do with real-world friendship, but rather are used as an indicator of popularity or sociability. The challenge for those making use of web analytics, like all web metrics, is to distinguish between those that are worth counting and those that are not.

As librarians make use of a greater range of online tools and services, there is an increasingly wide range of metrics that may be counted. This may be the number of views, favourites or comments a particular piece of content has received on a social network site such as Flickr, or how many visitors a site or page has received as viewed through Google Analytics.

As with link analysis, when investigating web analytics it is important to keep in mind that what is being counted should have been created individually and independently. Librarians could quite easily increase their number of Twitter followers by following the behaviour of many spam bots, automatically following accounts in the hope that they are reciprocally followed back. If they want to take precautions against this approach being recognized they can always unfollow the accounts a few days later. It should go without saying that this is not the recommended approach, but rather librarians should instead take steps to adjust their behaviour.

Relational web metrics

Relational metrics have generally received far less attention than evaluative metrics, although they too have a place within the work of librarians. Relational metrics are not about identifying the best or most appropriate resources, but rather providing an overview of the relationships between different actors; relational metrics may be used to provide maps of science. Typically such studies have made use of the elements available within bibliographic databases, usually through co-citation, co-word analysis or co-author analysis.

Computing technology has provided new impetus to relational bibliometrics as it enables the development of new tools to explore the maps (Noyons, 2001). Figure 2.2 shows a co-word analysis of the keywords that have been applied to webometric papers indexed by the Web of Science that has been simply created through the freely available computer program VOSviewer (www.vosviewer.com).

The web provides a host of new information sources about bibliographic resources. It is no longer necessary to restrict a co-word analysis to the data within established bibliometric databases; researchers can now make use of other online sources that refer to traditional publications. These include the use of bookmarking and reference managers, for example CiteULike

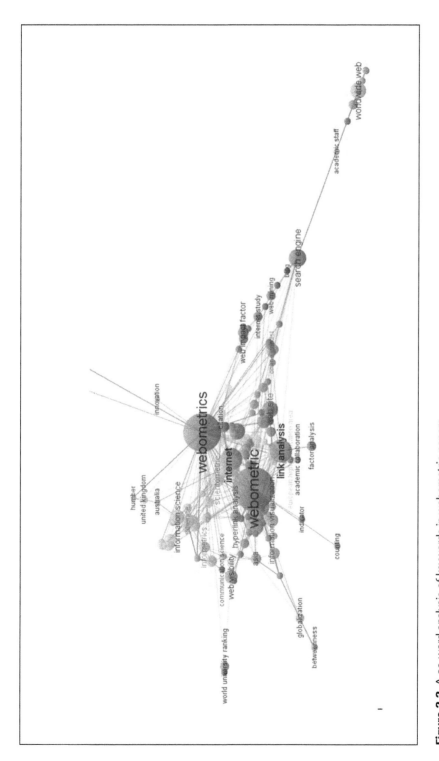

Figure 2.2 A co-word analysis of keywords in webometric papers

(www.citeulike.org) and Mendeley (www.mendeley.com), or even the subject headings and classifications that are available through the increasing availability of data from library catalogues.

The web also offers a host of information about non-bibliographic resources. Potentially offering insights into the relationships between organizations as they link online (Stuart and Thelwall, 2006) or communication (or lack of it) between political opponents in the blogosphere (Adamic and Glance, 2005).

While insights into these maps and graphs may be gleaned in some instances through viewing them, there is also a host of statistical methods from the field of social network analysis for analysing the roles of individual nodes within networks and the structure of the networks as a whole. Whereas many early webometric studies measured impact by the number of direct links a website received, where the data has been available for more of a network they have also taken into consideration other measures of centrality, such as betweenness and closeness (e.g., Ortega and Aguillo, 2008), which take into consideration whether a node is on the geodesics (shortest route) between other nodes and how close a node is to other nodes.

In some instances the difference between evaluative and relational web metrics is merely one of perspective. Yan, Ding and Zhu's (2010) co-authorship network analysis of library and information science in China found that the social network analysis value of centrality in a network was highly correlated with citation rankings. From a relational perspective centrality provides an understanding of the structure of the network; from an evaluative perspective centrality may provide an indicator of an author's impact in a field.

A librarian may use such mappings to provide a researcher new to a field with an overview of associated research, or to help those involved in policy identify emerging areas of research within a field. As more information about the scientific process is available online it is no longer necessary to restrict such relational investigations to those anchored in reference to traditional publications.

Validating the results

This book broadly follows Thelwall's (2004a) recommendation for link analysis: where possible conclusions from relational and evaluative web metrics investigations should be validated through a combination of correlation and categorization. The extent of such validation depends heavily on the purpose of the web metrics, and any actions that may be based on them.

Correlation

Testing to see whether a set of results correlates with an external measure of the inference that is being made is one of the most frequently applied statistical tests within webometrics. For example, for a set of companies a researcher may investigate whether the number of inlinks received by the companies' websites correlates with some other indicator of success such as their turnover, or whether the inlinks for a group of universities' websites correlate with the universities' research excellence. Generally such correlations are tested by calculating Spearman's rank coefficient, rather than Pearson's rank, as the distribution of inlinks, traffic and other web measures is often heavily skewed on the web.

Another important consideration when investigating whether one particular set of data correlates with something else is the sheer quantity of correlations that may be investigated. The web provides access to a huge variety of data on every conceivable topic, which raises the possibility of potentially drawing inappropriate conclusions from data, especially as the potential for automatic analysis and testing means that correlations may be found merely by searching for long enough. For example, many studies consider a correlation statistically significant if there is only a 1% or 5% chance of the correlation occurring at random. If only one set of data is tested, and it is found to be statistically significant, then the researcher may be fairly confident in their finding. However, if 100 different sets of data are tested and one is found to be statistically significant at the 1% level, then the researcher will necessarily be less confident in their finding. An established method for counteracting the increase in chance due to multiple comparisons is the Bonferroni correction, where each individual hypothesis is tested at a statistical significance level of 1 divided by the number of hypotheses tested multiplied by what it would be if only one hypothesis were tested. For example, if someone wants to be confident about a finding at the 1% level, and is testing ten hypotheses, then each should be tested for significance at the 0.1% level. This inevitably raises the difficulty in identifying statistically significant findings, which is why it is important to be selective in the choice of hypotheses that are tested rather than scouring the web for correlations.

As has often been noted, correlation and causation are two different things. Just because the number of inlinks a set of universities receives correlates with the institutions' research excellence, it does not mean that the links are placed because of the research excellence. It may be that the links are reflecting something else that also happens to correlate with the institutions' research excellence, for example, the size of the institution or its reputation for teaching. Mistaking one for the other might mean that some institutions are unfairly rewarded or penalized. Categorization can be used to add support for a correlation, or to investigate the reasons for instances of a web occurrence when correlation is not applicable.

Categorization

As has been regularly noted within bibliometric literature, citations are placed for many different reasons, and many different classification schemes have been proposed for the analysis of citations (Cronin, 1984). The same is true for web links, web mentions, or any other web phenomena that may form the basis of a web metric investigation. Links are placed to websites and organizations and individuals are mentioned for many different reasons, not all of which are complimentary or support the inference that a researcher may be trying to draw from the research. In fact, the wide variety of reasons for which web content is created, many of which are ill-defined and personal, are likely to be far more varied than the reasons for citation placement in academic publishing. Equally the reasons visitors arrive at a website may vary considerably.

As Marek (2011, 6) has stated: 'raw data only tells half the story'. For meaningful conclusions to be drawn from the data there needs to be a greater understanding of why it was created. It may be that a research project team wants to demonstrate the impact their project has made, and decides to use web mentions as an indicator. If the majority of web mentions revolve around criticisms of the funding agency financing such esoteric research in the first place, then web mentions are not necessarily a good indicator of the research's impact. It is therefore necessary for the research group to demonstrate that a significant proportion of the links has been placed for positive reasons. Equally, if a webometric study is trying to make the case that the number of web links can provide a useful indicator of the research value of an institution, the case is more forcibly made if it can be shown that a significant proportion of links are placed to reference research that is being carried out. As Sterne (2010) states in his work on social media metrics, 'true value comes from categorization' (186). Categorization allows a distinction to be made between those links or web mentions that are positive and those that are negative, those that are placed to reference a university's research, and those that are placed to highlight a gig at the student union.

Categorization in web metric research may be achieved through either sentiment analysis or content analysis. Sentiment analysis, or opinion mining, is generally used to refer to the automatic analysis of people's opinions about specific entities, whether people, events, goods, services or anything else people may have opinions about. It may be applied to a document, a sentence or specific aspects of entities (Feldman, 2013). The rapid growth in interest in sentiment analysis over the last decade has been driven and enabled by the vast quantities of opinionated data that is available online (Liu, 2012) as people increasingly express their opinions on every conceivable topic via social network sites and personal web pages. Content analysis, in comparison, does not limit itself to texts, but is the systematic analysis of any type of communication (including images and videos) and extends the range of questions that may be asked beyond the positive or negative (or neutral) opinion that is being expressed about an entity. The wider range of content, and questions that may be asked, occurs because content analysis is a human-centred approach to classifying the documents.

One methodology is not simply better than the other, but there are advantages and disadvantages to both sentiment analysis and content analysis, and the selection of one over the other depends on the nature of the investigation. The reasons why one methodology may be chosen over the other relate to either the nature of the content, or the nature of the enquiry.

Content may be more suitable for one form of analysis rather than another because of the content format, the content topic, the sample size, or the structure of the data source. People are going online in their millions to write reviews, share opinions, tweet observations, and upload images, videos and audio files. If a company wishes to know whether they are being represented positively or negatively among the thousands of images on Flickr they may be able to glean some insight from the comments or tags that have been applied to the photos, although primarily they will have to analyse the content itself. Although studies are increasingly finding automatic sentiment analysis to equate well with human sentiment analysis, one area where it continues to perform badly is with regards to sarcasm (Feldman, 2013); in this case, although humans may do better, sentiment analysis is nonetheless difficult because of the deficiencies of text as a medium. An obvious advantage of sentiment analysis is that it is an automated process, and within a few minutes a sentiment analysis program can have categorized thousands of texts that could have taken many hundreds or thousands of man hours. For example, when in an analysis of tweets sent during the H1N1 pandemic, although Chew and Eysenbach (2010) archived over 2 million tweets, the manual content analysis aspect involved only 5395 tweets. Alternatively, if an organization wants to respond whenever it is the subject of negative comments, if these make up a small proportion of the total number of comments then a level of automatic analysis may need to be included to identify the comments. However, if only a small number of pieces need to be analysed, it may be quicker to analyse the work manually than to carry out a sentiment analysis, especially if a domain specific lexicon needs to be created.

Structure of the information resource type is also important. Interest in sentiment analysis has not merely been driven by the growth of the web, but the growth of the structured content enabled by social media technologies. For example, Twitter enables access not only to huge amounts of content, but content that comes in distinct, discernible units. In comparison traditional web pages are messy, and identifying the relevant parts of a page for analysis may not be simply automated. Also, in many cases the person carrying out the analysis is not interested in the sentiment of a particular set of data, but rather some other question. For example, in the process of web analytics researchers may wish to determine whether the search terms used to arrive at their site were relevant to the site's core mission, something that cannot be determined from investigating whether the search terms are positive or negative.

Conclusion

This chapter has highlighted both the potential and the limitations of web metrics. They can provide new insights about the scientific process and traditional publication genres more widely, prove a useful research tool helping researchers to gain insights into the behaviour of individuals and groups, and provide a method for individuals and organizations to analyse their own online behaviour and reputation. However, there are also recognized limitations due to the tools, methodologies and nature of the web itself.

Even where findings are statistically significant it is important that the results are treated with caution. As is often noted, correlation is not the same as causation, and because of the ease with which data can be created online and the limitations of available tools, findings should be considered 'indicative rather than definitive' (Thelwall, 2009, 14).

Nonetheless, as can be concluded from this chapter, both evaluative and relational web metrics have a wide range of applications for librarians, some of the more useful of which are:

- measuring the impact of a library's content
- measuring the impact of library patron's content

- identifying important research and resources within a field
- supporting researchers with webometric investigations
- providing patrons with overviews of their research area.

3.

Data collection tools

Introduction

Like the library in Ranganathan's (1931) five laws of library science, the web is a growing organism, and the changing nature of the web is one of the themes that will be developed throughout this book. As this chapter will show, the technologies being utilized are changing, as are the sites and services available to investigate the web. Librarians need to understand the changing nature of such sites and services if they are to make use of web metrics for either relational or evaluative purposes.

Over the past 20 years the web has become a ubiquitous part of the modern world, and the development of associated tools and technologies has had a big impact on the nature of the web metric investigations that have taken place. During this period search engines have indexed large amounts of the web, and provided advanced search functionality that has enabled increasingly complex investigations of web content and hyperlink networks. The Web 2.0 revolution saw the major search engines and social media services provide application programming interfaces (APIs) so that developers could automatically interact with a website's content, enabling larger scale investigations to take place. The establishing of semantic web standards promised a web where many of people's mundane computing tasks could be completed automatically by computer programs (Berners-Lee, Hendler and Lassila, 2001), while the development of cookies has enabled organizations to track users both within and across websites (Turow, 2011). However, technological progress has not been smooth and uninterrupted. Search engine and API functionality has in some instances been retracted, a semantic web has not emerged as quickly as some people expected, and restrictions have been placed on cookies by the European Commission (Information Commission Office, 2012). All these changes have had an effect on the types of web metrics that can be developed: those metrics that were available yesterday may not be available tomorrow, but new ones will emerge. Understanding how the tools have changed in the past can help us to understand how they may change in the future and help us to recognize potential areas of opportunity.

Unless researchers gather information from the web manually, they need tools to gather the information on their behalf, and in the less than two decades since the first paper that may be considered webometric (Larson, 1996) there have been four distinct periods for webometric research tools. After first introducing the necessary terminology for describing web documents and the linking between them, the chapter discusses the changing nature of the tools that have formed the basis of webometric research within the information science community. Webometrics is not about specific tools but paradigms through which researchers view the web. Although this book is not focused solely on webometrics, but also web bibliometrics, web scientometrics and web analytics, many of the tools discussed are of use within each situation; while an extensive history of all tools associated with web metrics would quickly have become unwieldy and taken up much of the book.

The anatomy of a URL, web links and the structure of the web

The phenomena that form the basis of web metric investigations do not have to be explicit hyperlinks between documents, but may be based on less explicit relationships, such as shared terms, phrases, languages or document types. Nevertheless, much of the conversation about the changing nature of the tools for webometric analysis and the depreciation of functionality is reliant on an understanding of the structure of URLs and the linking structure of the web itself.

The URL is one of the basic units of the web and many webometric studies, and when discussing web pages, sub-domains or websites the concepts are generally operationalized through their URLs. It is not the only way the concepts could be operationalized; web pages could be clustered into web documents or sites according to the content of the pages, or the interlinking between pages (Cothey, Aguillo and Arroyo, 2006). However, the URL may be considered the most intuitive and easiest way to operationalize these concepts and it forms the basis of most webometric investigations.

The URL itself can comprise a number of different parts: a protocol, a username, a password, a domain name, a port, a query and an anchor. Although URLs occasionally include usernames and passwords, and decisions about how to deal with dynamically generated content (the query part of a URL) may need to be made, the most important terminology of URLs used throughout this book is illustrated in Figure 3.1.

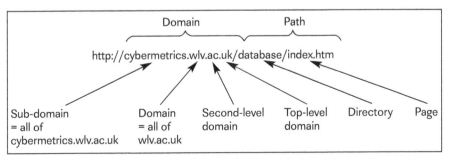

Figure 3.1 An example of a URL labelled with the link analysis terminology

The structure of the URLs have enabled webometric investigations to make use of the interlinking between different web documents, which may be operationalized at top-level domains, second-level domains, domains, sub-domains, as well as directories and pages. The top-level domains (TLDs) were traditionally restricted to a small number of generic TLDs (gTLDs) (e.g., .com, .org, .gov and .edu) and country-code TLDs (ccTLDs). Some ccTLDs have also been further broken down into second-level domain names (e.g., .ac.uk and .co.uk), although not all countries make use of a second-level domain name system (e.g., .fr).

The structure has been used in link analysis to investigate the interlinking between types of institution (e.g., making use of gTLDs) and between countries (e.g., making use of ccTLDs). An increase in the number of gTLDs is expected in 2013 as the Internet Corporation for Assigned Names and Numbers (ICANN) has invited applications for new TLDs from organizations. We may soon have URLs such as http://news.bbc or http://pubs.london. Most inter-document investigations have taken place at the domain level, for example looking at the interlinking between the domains of universities or commercial organizations, although in some instances the sub-domain, directory or page may be a more appropriate operationalization of the web document. For example, blogs on the Blogger blogging platforms make use of sub-domains for different blogs (e.g., http://googleblog. blogspot.co.uk) and as these generally have distinct authors and purposes it makes sense to treat the different sub-domains as different websites.

Webometric investigations investigate not only the documents, but also the inter-document connections between web documents. Even when restricting ourselves to the placement of hyperlinks, rather than any other type of inter-document connection, different linking terminology has been used. While a hyperlink describes the placing of a link within the HTML of one document, the page that is the focus of that link has been variously described as having a hypertext citation (Chen et al., 1998), a sitation (Rousseau, 1997) or a backlink (Harter and Ford, 2000), a term that continues to be popular within the search engine optimization community. This book follows the terminology of Björneborn and Ingwersen (2004):

- An *outlink* occurs where a link is placed within a web document that points to a URL outside the web document.
- An *inlink* is where a hyperlink from outside a web document refers to a place within a web document.
- A *self-link* refers to a link within a web document pointing to a place within a web document, for example, if web documents are operationalized at the domain level, one page within the domain linking to another page within the domain would be considered a self-link.
- A *reciprocal-link* occurs where two web documents link to one another, although this does not necessarily have to be the same two pages linking to one another.

As well as understanding how different web documents have been operationalized through the use of URLs, and understanding the terminology for different inter-document linking, it is necessary to place webometric research within the context of the structure of the web as a whole. Figure 3.2 shows Broder et al.'s (2000) web connectivity model. This helps us to understand how websites connect to one another, and the implications the uni-directional nature of web links have on what may be known about the web.

Broder et al.'s (2000) 'bow tie' model is based on two crawls of the web by the AltaVista search engine, which consisted of over 200 million web pages and 1.5 billion web links. Web pages can be classified as falling within one of a number of distinct categories according to how they link to the web as a whole. The strongly connected component (SCC) represents the core of the web, a highly connected set of pages which may be reached by any other page within the strongly connected component through following a path of links. The IN component includes pages that can reach the strongly connected

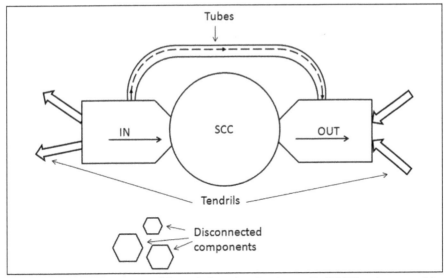

Figure 3.2 The link structure of the web, based on Broder et al.'s (2000) web connectivity model

component, but cannot be reached from it, while the OUT component includes pages which can be reached from the strongly connected component but from which the strongly connected component cannot be reached. There are also pages that are connected to the IN and/or from the OUT component, but are not connected to the strongly connected component, as well as disconnected components that are not connected to the strongly connected component, the IN component or the OUT component.

The structure of the web has important ramifications when considering tools for investigating the web. If the starting points for investigating the web are all taken from the disconnected components, or the OUT component, then nothing can be known about the IN component, the strongly connected component, other disconnected components, tubes or certain tendrils. This structure emphasizes the importance of having multiple starting points for a crawl of the web, and if many of the disconnected components are going to be found the website owners must want them to be found. The structure emphasizes the importance of search engines to webometric research.

Search engines 1.0

Search engines have provided one of the most important sources of information for webometric investigations since the earliest webometric papers (e.g., Larson, 1996; Rousseau, 1997; Ingwersen, 1998). They provide a ready source of information that can be quickly gathered either from manually entering queries or scraping results (automatically extracting the data that is required from the downloaded HTML page). AltaVista was particularly popular in early investigations as its link functionality allowed the investigation of how websites linked to a particular page or domain. Studies making use of its link functionality included evaluative investigations into the impact of websites (e.g., Smith, 1999) and relational investigations into the connectivity between universities, industry and government (Boudourides, Sigrist and Alevizos, 1999) and general top-level domain names (Thelwall, 2001a).

Today's major search engines (e.g., Bing and Google) index far more of the web than would be possible by any individual researcher or research group, for various reasons: indexing the web requires huge amounts of processing power and bandwidth; online documents can come in multiple different formats; and it is in the interests of website owners to ensure that their content has been indexed by the search engines.

Search engines make use of web crawlers, also known as spiders or robots; these are programs that automatically download pages from the web. Starting with a seed list of URLs, each of the pages referred to by the URLs is downloaded, and any URLs embedded within those web pages are extracted and added to the queue of URLs to be downloaded. This process is then repeated in an iterative fashion until as much of the web has been downloaded as required. Different web crawlers may make use of different crawling strategies, prioritizing the downloading of certain web pages over others, or only indexing part of the downloaded page. The web is not only vast but also constantly growing and changing, making it difficult to index any more than a small part of it. While it is meaningless to ask about the exact size of the web as so many pages are created dynamically and do not exist until they are called, Google claims it has identified 30 trillion unique URLs and crawls 20 billion of those on an average day (Sullivan, 2012).

These web pages are encoded not solely in a standard HTML format, but also in a wide variety of other formats, from Flash to Microsoft Word documents. Google indexes a wide variety of documents in addition to HTML (Google, 2013), although such extensive web crawler development is likely to be beyond the individual or small research group.

Equally importantly, while it is in the interests of website owners to make sure their website's content is indexed by search engines, site owners may not only be uninterested in having their content indexed by a researcher's web crawler, but even take steps to prevent a researcher's web crawler crawling a site. A web page can only be found if it is linked to by another web page, and the structure of the web means that there are many web pages that are either disconnected or link to the strongly connected core of the web but are not linked to from it (Broder et al., 2000). Although website owners may choose to submit their website or page for indexing by a major search engine such as Google, they may actually want to discourage web crawling by researchers and make use of the robots' exclusion standard to express the fact that they do not want to be crawled by unknown web crawlers. As a large amount of crawling may have a significant impact on a small website, with no discernible benefit to the website owner, it is important for researchers to take an ethical approach to crawling the web. This includes respecting the robots' exclusion standards, and those sites that have not included a robot exclusion standard also taking reasonable precautions (Thelwall and Stuart, 2006).

There are, however, disadvantages in making use of a search engine's crawl data to investigate the links between websites. These include issues regarding coverage, transparency, reliability, link functionality and the ability to retrieve all results. Although search engines cover far more of the web than most researchers would be able to gather for themselves, search engines do not crawl the whole web. Partly this is because of technical limitations (the problem of identifying all of Broder et al.'s (2000) 'disconnected components'), and partly the result of decisions that are made in the prioritizing of crawling certain sections of the web (e.g., prioritizing pages in English at the top of websites). The webometric researcher does not know what the crawling policy of a search engine is; to keep a competitive edge search engines lack transparency. It is important for webometric researchers to know what has been crawled, and how a search engine ranks results and estimates the number of results that it has found. The estimated number of results for a particular query often diverges wildly from the actual number of results a search engine can provide the reader with access to. For example, a Google phrase search for the title of the book *Facilitating Access to the Web of Data* has about 12,300 results. However, if one clicks through the pages of results one comes to an abrupt halt at page 15, and a message declares that there are only 146 results that have been found that match the query. This reliability issue can have serious implications for webometric research as search engines generally limit the number of results that may be viewed (e.g., to 1000). Thus for most queries there is no way of determining the actual number of results, they are merely rough estimates. The limited number of results not only limits the precision of the number of results found, but also has implications for validating conclusions through the use of content analysis. Content analysis cannot be based on a random sample from all matching results, but must necessarily be based on the 1000 results, which may skew the results.

As well as limitations with the results, there are also limitations with the queries that can be sent to a search engine. Although search engines like Google allow for the use of a number of advanced searching functionalities, such as phrase searching and Boolean operators (e.g., AND, OR, NOT) and the restricting of results according to region, language, document type and even reading level of material, and previously provided limited link search functionality, there is a lot of functionality that is not available. When link searching was available it was operationalized at the page or domain level; it was not possible to search for links pointing to sub-domains or directories. Keyword and phrase search also does not allow for the same complexity of queries that could be expressed through regular expressions (regex). For example, there is no way to ask Google to return all pages with an e-mail address as there is no way to express the concept of an e-mail address in Google's search box, although the structure of an e-mail address may be expressed as a regular expression, which allows the expression of character patterns.

These limitations may be partly attributable to protecting their intellectual property, and partly due to the limitations of indexing. It would be impossible to index the web for every possible regex query, instead it is necessary for a regex query to be matched against a particular set of data. For this it is necessary that the researcher has their own copy of the data.

Web crawlers

Although researchers may not have the ability to crawl the whole of the web for themselves, they can crawl part of it. There are a number of web crawlers freely available to researchers, including the Internet Archive's Heritrix (http://crawler.archive.org) and the Statistical Cybermetrics Research Group's SocSciBot (http://socscibot.wlv.ac.uk). The development of SocSciBot, a web crawler specifically for webometric purposes (Thelwall, 2001b), provided access to far more reliable data about the linking and content of websites.

By using a web crawler a webometric researcher can specify the parameters of the data they want included within a crawl, and crawl as much or as little of the web as they wish. It is also expected that every time the same set of data is queried, the same results will be found. That is not to say there is no ambiguity with data from a web crawl: different web crawlers may collect different data as they are able to extract different links, and even if the web pages themselves have not changed, unresponsive servers may mean that different versions of the web are available. A far wider range of search queries may be created than is possible through a regular search engine, including link searches. From the perspective of good scientific practice, it is possible for the data set that has been investigated to be shared, either by making it available online, or to those who ask for it.

Many web crawler studies have focused on the UK academic web space (e.g., Thelwall and Price, 2003; Thelwall, Harries and Wilkinson, 2003), as the UK academic web space is small enough to be crawled by a research group and it is a sufficiently large web space to be of interest and offers the opportunity for correlation tests to be carried out between web impact and the RAE.

Although web crawlers enabled far more reliable investigations to focus on a smaller area of the web, increased functionality from the search engines in the form of APIs, which facilitate access to their large quantity of data, swung webometric interest back in their favour.

Search engines 2.0

In 2002 Google started to provide an API for automatic access to its search engine, and this was soon followed by Yahoo! and Live Search (as Microsoft's search engine was named at the time). As all three search engines also allowed the identification of links to either a specific page or domain, they provided the potential for webometric studies that included a far larger set of websites than could be crawled with a personal crawler. Although search engines continued to have many of the limitations previously identified in reliability, transparency, possible queries and the ability to retrieve all results, the APIs seemingly tipped the scales back in the search engine's favour for webometric research. The search engine APIs have formed the basis of many webometric studies, both relational (e.g., Stuart and Thelwall, 2007) and evaluative (e.g., Kousha and Thelwall, 2008). However, the search engine advantage was relatively short lived. Link functionality has been retracted, and APIs turned off.

Whereas once the links between websites could be investigated using the link functionality of search engines, it has been necessary to investigate the potential of other types of linking. While the development of APIs by search engines for automatic processing of search engine content was a boon to webometric research, by May 2011 Bing Search API 2.0 was identified as the only source for webometric research from a major search engine suitable for offline processing (Thelwall and Sud, 2012). At the time of writing, Bing includes no inbuilt link functionality and users are restricted to 5000 queries a month.

The priorities of the commercial search engines are not the same as the priorities of those who are trying to use them as research tools. Inconsistent results, inconsistent search engine operators, and hidden crawling and ranking policies do little to detract from an average user's experience of a search engine, although consistency and openness would be extremely valuable to the researcher.

Unfortunately no search engine comes close to meeting the specifications of an ideal search engine for webometric research that others have identified (e.g., Bar-Ilan, 2005), although they continue to have a role in webometric research as researchers adjust their methodologies to the limitations of the tools that are available. For example, recent webometric papers have included an investigation into whether the number of web pages on which a company's name appears has been found to correlate with the company's revenue, profits and assets (Vaughan and Romero-Frías, 2012), and a content analysis of Korean and Chinese web pages was used to discover similarities and differences in the way the web is used in the two countries (Hsu and Park, 2012a). Increasingly, however, we have moved to a fragmentation of research tools.

Post Search Engine 2.0: fragmentation

We have now moved into a Post Search Engine 2.0 age with no single dominant webometric tool. Instead webometric researchers are constantly looking for new sources of data, as well as returning to previous tools, while also investigating alternatives to the hyperlink as an indicator of impact or relationship.

Search engines and alternative links: URL citations and web mentions

Hyperlinks are not the only indicator of impact, and the reduction of link analysis functionality from search engines has led to increased interest in alternative methods of calculating impact making use of the extensive crawls of the popular search engines.

One such indicator has been the number of URL citations, because of its similarity with hyperlinks. The URL citations of a web page are defined as 'the mentions of its URL in the test of other Web pages, whether hyperlinked or not' (Kousha and Thelwall, 2006). All URL citations to a site may be calculated by carrying out a phrase search for a URL and excluding those citations within the same site. For example:

www.bbc.co.uk −site:bbc.co.uk

URL citations may also be used for relational web metrics. For example, Stuart and Thelwall (2006) investigated whether co-operation between universities, government and commercial organizations in the West Midlands in the UK was visible through URL citations between the sites. For example, URL mentions of the Wolverhampton Council website on the University of Wolverhampton website:

www.wolverhampton.gov.uk site:wlv.ac.uk

There are a number of problems with URL citations, however. It is only an indicator of the number of hyperlinks, and search engines' results have been found to be unreliable (Thelwall and Sud, 2011). Nevertheless they continue to be investigated as a potential source of impact (e.g., Orduña-Malea and Regazzi, 2013).

The web mentions of a particular phrase may also be investigated. A web impact assessment is the measuring of the impact of a resource or an idea through evaluating how often they are mentioned online (Thelwall, 2009); this idea is investigated more fully in Chapter 7 where the methodology is applied to bibliometric resources. Co-mentions may also be investigated; for example, Chung and Park (2012) investigated the visibility of authors on their own and their networked visibility by investigating whether scholars' names appeared together.

APIs and web scrapers

It is not necessary for webometric research to revolve solely around the data that is available by the search engines. Many of the most influential websites have been the subject of webometric investigations either through the authorized use of a website's data via its API or through unauthorized access to the data via a web scraper. Two of the key principles of the Web 2.0 revolution were the importance of data and harnessing collective intelligence (O'Reilly, 2005), and many of the dominant Web 2.0 sites and services made it possible to collect data from their services automatically, which has then formed the basis of academic investigations: Twitter (e.g., Stuart, 2010; Choi, Park and Park, 2012; Wilkinson and Thelwall, 2012), Flickr (e.g., Angus, Thelwall and Stuart, 2008), YouTube (e.g., Benevenuto et al., 2008) and Digg (Paltoglou, Thelwall and Buckley, 2010).

Most sites find it less easy to extract the data, however, and bespoke tools have needed to be created for extracting the required information from certain sites, for example MySpace (Thelwall, 2008) and comments on the BBC website (Paltoglou, Thelwall and Buckley, 2010). Where an API is not available, web scrapers may be used. A web scraper is similar to a web crawler, although rather than downloading the unstructured HTML content of the web page they are designed for extracting specific content from the web. For example a web scraper may be designed to extract the comments from a particular newspaper website or the posts on a social networking site. There is also a dynamic community of scrapers available at ScraperWiki (http://scraperwiki.com). The site provides a web-based platform where programmers can create code that is run automatically and the data is stored. Even if someone finds that the data has not already been scraped and they do not have the requisite skills to write the scraping program themselves, there is also the option to request data: you can pay someone to scrape the data for you.

The development of software to either automatically extract the data from a website's API or to scrape the content from the website itself is likely to be beyond the ability of many researchers; as Giles (2012) has noted, while social scientists have many interesting questions to ask, they often lack the necessary methodological skills of computer scientists to collect and interrogate large quantities of data.

The provision of data via an API gives the publishing website more control over the content: they may restrict access levels, which content they share via the API, and they do not have to give away all their content. In many situations this is also useful to the end-user. For example, even if a search engine was willing to share all the content that they had gathered in one gigantic file it would be likely to be of little use to most potential users!

Although APIs can provide interesting insights into web use, they provide a disjointed vision of the web. It would be useful if APIs structured their content in the same way, according to widespread standards, and with unique identifiers to refer to individual records. Such an approach is a vision of the semantic web. The semantic web, and the development of tools specifically for webometric investigations, cannot rightly be considered a distinct stage in the history of webometric research yet. It does, however, offer the potential for a new paradigm of webometric research in the future, potentially bringing the currently dispersed fragments back together, and it is returned to in Chapter 8.

Data aggregators

There are now additional tools, data aggregators for want of a better term, that provide insights into one particular data type. Although search engines seem to be as far from the webometric ideal search engine as they have ever been, if not further, they have developed a number of additional tools, most noticeably in Google. As with its search engine functionality, the Google product line is in a regular state of flux, with the average service lasting just short of four years (Arthur, 2013) and tools that may once have proved useful to webometric research have been discontinued. These are Google's Social Graph API, which indexed social relationships expressed according to two widespread mark-up standards, and was retired in April 2012; and Google Insights for Search, which provided insights into the search terms entered into Google, and was merged with Google Trends in September 2012.

As the Western world's most popular search engine, announcing in August 2012 that it handled 100 billion searches per month (Sullivan, 2012), Google has the potential to provide insights into the content that is available online, and a number of tools to provide insights into what people are searching for. Google Trends (www.google.com/trends) provides a simple way to see the variation in search volume for a particular term over time. For example, Figure 3.3 shows the volume of searches that included 'how to':

Figure 3.3 shows that the number of 'how to' searches was fairly steady from January 2004 until the end of 2007, since when it has risen steadily. It would seem a reasonable starting hypothesis that the financial crisis of

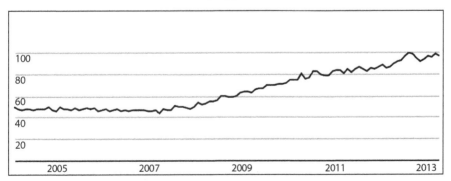

Figure 3.3 Proportion of Google searches that included the term 'how to' according to Google Trends, 2005–2013 [Google and the Google logo are registered trademarks of Google Inc., used with permission]

2007–2008, and the subsequent global recession, increased the number of people trying to do tasks for themselves rather than using professionals. Although Google cannot tell us why individuals started to enter these search terms at this particular time, it does allow further breakdown according to regional searches which, coupled with additional information about individual economies, may or may not provide supporting evidence. In a similar manner, Pries et al. (2012) have used Google Trends to show that internet users from countries with a higher GDP are more likely to search for information about the future than the past.

That search behaviour can reflect real-world activities has been most famously demonstrated in Google Flu Trends (www.google.org/flutrends), where Google uses aggregated search data to estimate flu activity. It has been suggested that such trends could aid the early detection of an outbreak, and thus help reduce the number of people affected. Following the success of Google Flu Trends, Google released Google Correlate (www.google.com/trends/correlate) as a tool to help identify the terms that correspond with a particular phenomenon.

Conclusion

The web will undoubtedly continue to change in the future; like the library it is a growing organism and librarians wanting to make use of web metrics will undoubtedly have to accept that change is inevitable. The sites and technologies encountered within this book will change, but the principles will not. At the moment Facebook, Twitter and LinkedIn dominate much of the discussion of social network sites, and are understandably of interest to librarians wishing to measure their impact. However, as has already been seen, leading social media sites quickly come and go, and there is nothing to say that the current crop will not follow in the footsteps of previous leading social network sites that have fallen out of fashion, such as Friendster and MySpace (Boyd and Ellison, 2007), let alone offer the same functionality. Librarians need to recognize the types of information that may be useful, the types of tools that are likely to be available, and some of the potential limitations of web metrics.

Webometric research today is undoubtedly epitomized by the lack of a single tool, and the broader area of web metrics even more so. While this undoubtedly allows for a far wider variety of investigations than would be possible with earlier web metric methodologies, current methodologies are rarely focused on the big picture. They also require researchers to use a wide set of tools, and while these tools are the focus of the next five chapters, it is important to keep the changing nature of the tools and technologies in mind.

4

Evaluating impact on the web

Introduction

The web provides the opportunity for metrics to be used for a wide range of investigations, most of which may be broadly categorized as either evaluative or relational. This chapter broadly considers evaluative metrics for websites, blogs and other self-hosted content, Chapter 5 considers evaluative metrics for third-party social media services that a large number of individuals and organizations make use of, and Chapter 6 considers relational web metrics. In many ways the split between self-hosted and third-party hosted content is an artificial one. For example, millions of blogs are hosted on third-party sites such as Blogger.com, while individuals and organizations do not have to rely on a microblogging service such as Twitter, but could host their own microblogging service using open source software such as Status.net (http://status.net). The split reflects a significant difference in the control a user has over the data that is available and an uncertainty in the data that is collected.

When people or organizations host their own content on their own servers the only limitations of the information that they gather about the use of content on their site are technical problems to be overcome. However, when a website is integrated into the wider ecosystem there is more uncertainty: in the same way that there is no simple answer to how many web pages exist, there is not a simple answer to how many links a website has pointing to it or how many times it is mentioned. This is a problem that is made more difficult as the web is necessarily viewed through the limited view of a particular search engine or other tool, and the limitations of the tool are not always explicit. In comparison many of the large social network sites provide a restricted environment, where only certain behaviour is allowed (because of editorial and technical restrictions) and only certain data may be accessed.

These restrictions also reduce the ambiguity in the data available from the services; a Twitter account has a known number of followers, a Facebook user has a known number of friends, a YouTube video has a known number of views. We may disagree with the concept of Facebook's 'Like' button or what counts as a view on YouTube, but these are known discernible units.

Relational web metrics invariably require the evaluation of data from third-party sites and services, and although the analysis may differ, many of the same tools may be used for data collection.

This chapter considers the types of hosted content most likely to be found on the web (websites, blogs and wikis), and the types of information that librarians may be interested in gathering for evaluative purposes. It then takes a closer look at the main method for analysing content from a wide variety of sites: content analysis.

Websites

Most website owners take steps to measure their online impact in some way, shape or form. Hit counters may be far less prominent now than they once were, as the idiosyncratic personal home page has made way for the corporate blandness and good design of the social networking site, but most individuals and organizations with websites have nevertheless taken steps to capture information about the impact their content is having. They may not pay as much attention to this data as they should, settling instead for whichever method requires the least ongoing commitment and then failing to bother to read the data, but the potential value of this data is widely recognized by most website owners for web analytic purposes. Unless a website owner takes steps to measure how people are interacting with their website they cannot be sure whether a site is meeting its objectives, in fact they cannot be sure if anyone is even visiting the website! These objectives vary considerably depending on the type of website.

The simplest website may be a single page of text: no links, nothing to click, merely words on a page. Yet even for such a simple page the website administrator wants to know how many people are reading the content. As they cannot look over each visitor's shoulder to check whether they are actually reading the content, or indeed whether more than one person is reading the content at a time, they most likely accept the number of times the web pages is requested from the server as an indicator of the number of visitors, although this is by no means the limit to the metrics. The administrator may gather data on how people are accessing the site, whether by search engine or clicking on a link on an external site. They may be interested in the number of people who are return visitors, or the operating system or browser that they use as it may give an insight into the type of user.

With even the simplest of websites there is already a battery of metrics from which a website administrator may build their case for the impact (or lack thereof) of their site: that a site has not had as many viewers as expected may be compensated for by the fact that those visitors they did receive were primarily high-end users, as indicated by Apple operating systems. The larger than expected number of visitors may be tempered by the fact that they reached the web page via search engine terms that, while included within the text of the page, were incidental to its primary content. As a website gets more complex so does the potential for the metrics which are captured. Multiple pages raise questions about which pages users are landing on, how many pages they are visiting, and the amount of time they are spending on each page. Wherever there is room for interaction there is room for additional metrics: how many times has the online survey been answered? How many e-mails have been received? For the most part the interaction on a traditional website is of secondary importance, but with social media it is of primary importance.

Blogs

Social media has been defined as 'Internet-based applications that build on the ideological and technological foundations of Web 2.0, and that allow the creation and exchange of User Generated Content' (Kaplan and Haenlein, 2010, 61), and while this definition includes the dominant social networking sites such as Flickr, Twitter and Facebook, as well as collaboratively created content such as Wikipedia, it may also include personal instances such as a blog or even a hosted wiki. As with the traditional website, information may be gathered about the users reading or visiting the content, but social media is not merely about publishing content, but interacting with visitors and receiving feedback.

Blogs, regularly updated websites displaying pages in reverse chronological order, are one of the longest established social media technologies with the term first being applied in 1997 and an explosion of blogs emerging following the launch of free web-based blogging software in 1999 (Blood, 2000). They have now been widely adopted by every conceivable type of organization and by individuals sharing every conceivable piece of information from their lives. Libraries have not been immune to the lure of blogging, and blogs can be found that are associated with libraries and information services from every sector, while many librarians also host their own blogs. Although there has been a decline in blogging in recent years, much of which may be attributable to the rise of social network sites such as Twitter and Facebook, nonetheless a core set of blogs by librarians persists (Torres-Salinas, Cabezas-Clavijo and Ruiz-Perez, 2011).

The broad definition of a blog used above hides one of the most significant distinguishing features of the blog: the comment. Most people still consider a blog to be a blog irrespective of whether or not the blog allows comments, although it is the comments that distinguish the blog from just another content management system; without comments blogging software achieves little more than what could be accomplished (albeit with considerably more effort) through the creation of HTML files in a text editor. Comments provide the opportunity for a conversation with the visitors of a website, to discover whether they are returning to the website because a post is considered good or merely well received. It may be that the comments rather than the more abstract number of users are particularly important for librarians: to have 100 visitors to a website in a day may be less important than ten visitors who are commenting and responding to requests for feedback, especially if the comments are classified according to the type of comment, such as 'positive feedback on new resources', 'suggestions for improvements' or even 'criticisms'. Although criticisms in most cases are unlikely to be welcomed with open arms, and in many cases they may be unfounded, the comment option nevertheless offers a useful channel for users to air their grievances. In the long run, comments may also provide an indicator of an improvement of service as the proportion of criticisms goes down as a percentage of overall blog comments.

Wikis

The wiki, another social media that an institution or individual may host for themselves, has been adopted to a far lesser degree than the blog, at least on the open web. Wikis have been defined as 'web-based software that allows all viewers of a page to change the content by editing the page online in a browser' (Ebersbach, Glaser and Heigl, 2008). The most famous example of a wiki is Wikipedia (http://en.wikipedia.org), the free encyclopedia that anyone can edit. The crowd-sourced approach to the creation of web documents has both advantages and disadvantages. On the one hand documents may be created – potentially for free – on a scale that would be impossible otherwise:

the 4,164,871 articles in English that Wikipedia claims dwarfs the size of a traditional encyclopedia, such as *Encyclopaedia Britannica*. Wikis also provide the opportunity to gain a wide range of perspectives on a topic. However, the articles that are created are created for those areas that users are interested in, not those areas that may be considered important by an editorial committee. This means that in the case of Wikipedia some areas are far more extensive than others; for example, the Star Trek series and the Star Trek universe are extensively detailed, with articles created for every episode, race, character and even spaceship!

Wikis can be subject to vandalism and misinformation, although in general a well used wiki seems to abide to the information equivalent of Linus's Law from the open source software community: 'Given enough eyeballs, all bugs are shallow' (Raymond, 2001, 30); given enough eyeballs all errors in information will be short lived. Nonetheless, as the distribution of interest in articles is likely to be uneven, and some articles are more likely to be prone to vandalism than others, not all vandalism is quickly detected. Probably the most famous case of wiki-vandalism was when the article about the journalist John Seigenthaler was changed to suggest he had been a suspect in the assassinations of both John F. Kennedy and Robert Kennedy, and the vandalism went unchanged for a number of months (Journalism.org, 2005). Nonetheless, despite an estimated 14,000 vandal edits every day (Mola-Velasco and Rosso, 2011), in studies some years ago Wikipedia was found to compare well to *Encyclopaedia Britannica* in a comparison of scientific articles (Giles, 2005), and in a comparison with Medscape Drug Reference no factual errors were identified, although Wikipedia was not found to be as extensive as a traditional edited database (Clauson et al., 2008). When a comparison of historical articles was made with other sources it was found to compare less well (Rector, 2008), however. Such studies emphasize the greater vulnerability of certain types of article to misinformation over others, but rather than dismiss the potential of collaborative projects such as Wikipedia, they demonstrate the need for a large number of responsible editors. In recent years there has been an initiative to improve the relationship between Wikimedia, the organization that runs Wikipedia, and libraries, with wiki-workshops and edit-athons in 2011 and 2012 (Wikipedia, 2013b).

Within the library community itself there are relatively few active wikis in comparison with other social media technologies. This may be seen as part of the difficulty in sustaining an active wiki. These are some of those that are publicly accessible, and have been active for a number of years:

- *Library Success* (www.libsuccess.org) – a best practice guide of ideas and information for the library community; at the time of writing (summer 2013) the front page has received over 1 million views
- *LISwiki* (http://liswiki.org) – a general wiki for library and information science, the front page of which has received over 300,000 views
- *SJCPL subject guides* (www.libraryforlife.org/subjectguides) – a wiki by St Joseph County Public Library, aimed at the general public rather than librarians; the front page has been viewed almost half a million times.

Each of these wiki makes use of MediaWiki (www.mediawiki.org) software and has been active since 2005, the year Writely was launched, a web-based word processor that was later acquired by Google and incorporated into Google Docs, allowing the collaborative editing of a document. These developments have made wikis a somewhat niche product, as many of the collaborative products for which they may once have been useful can now be accomplished more easily with a collaborative word processing document. However, there continue to be many places where wiki software, such as the proprietary software Confluence, is used for internal organizational purposes, and wikis also provide a useful tool for open notebook science (e.g., the Bradley Laboratory at Drexel University's open notebook science project in chemistry at http://usefulchem.wikispaces.com). Therefore many librarians may need to consider wiki metrics for the purpose of web analytics or even scientometric purposes.

As with the establishment of metrics for blogs, wikis are about interaction and collaboration, and it is important to establish metrics that measure these factors. The specific metrics are likely to vary considerably depending on the purpose of the wiki or wiki article; some articles and wikis may be more person-focused while others may be more content-focused. Public librarians wishing to elicit feedback on how to improve their service may wish to retrieve feedback from as wide a range of members as possible, and the number of contributors is all important. If the purpose of a wiki is to build a useful resource, however, then it may be the number of pages (or at least the number of pages over a particular size) that is important. In other cases the number of edits that a page has received might be considered particularly important; Wilkinson and Huberman (2007) identified a correlation between article quality and the number of edits.

A distinction should be made between the quality of the article and the quality of the object that is being described: at the time of writing the Wikipedia page for the 2003 novel *The Da Vinci Code* had been edited 5647 times, while the Man Booker Prize winner of the same year, *Vernon God Little*, had been edited a mere 173 times. As will be seen in Chapter 7, user behaviour on Wikipedia can provide insights into real-world behaviour.

These are all internal metrics, the information is either contained within the website itself (e.g., the number of comments on a blog or the number of edits on a wiki) or software has been set up to collect specific information that may be available only to the website owners (e.g., page views and traffic sources). There are also potential external metrics that are not dependent on the decisions of individual websites to collect or share data, but may be viewed about websites across the web. These metrics may not only provide additional insights for website owners for web analytical purposes, but also allow for scientometric, bibliometric and webometric investigations.

The primary importance of external metrics for web analytics is to provide context for information that an individual may already be able to gather for themselves. Librarians may already know that their blog receives 500 visits a day, but they have little idea of whether this is good or bad without the context of the number of visits other similar institutions receive. They may also have little understanding of why they are receiving traffic: is the content being discussed in a positive or a negative fashion? Has a website or content been linked with a current news story or promoted by a site with particularly high levels of traffic? Although some of this information is available through internal metrics, browsers have increasingly taken steps to enable users to hide some of their online behaviour (Sullivan, 2013).

Equally important, external metrics also provide the opportunity for scientometric and webometric investigations. In most situations the websites, blogs and wikis hosted by librarians are unlikely to provide sufficiently large data sets to draw scientometric or webometric conclusions. Instead it is necessary to draw patterns from data more widely.

Internal metrics

Internal metrics are not the primary focus of this book as these have already been the focus of many other far more detailed works, including Kate Marek's (2011) 'Using Web Analytics in the Library', which as the title suggests is aimed specifically at the community of librarians. It is also likely to be the case for many within the library profession that there is little choice about the data that is collected as they may be reliant on content management systems that belong to the wider organization, and may even be restricted in the information that the IT services department are willing to share.

Internal metrics are only dealt with briefly here. First, a brief overview of Google Analytics and log analysis is provided to give librarians an idea of the type of data that may be collected, how it is collected, and some of the current issues surrounding the collection of such data. This is not designed to provide advice on implementing an extensive web analytics program, but rather to give librarians an idea of what is possible, and the data they may reasonably ask their IT services to give them access to if they do not have access to the data themselves.

This is followed by a brief discussion of wikimetrics. The data that is available depends heavily on the software that is being used, although tools have been built that provide established web metrics (e.g., page views) for wiki-based content and more wiki-centric concepts (e.g., number of editors or edits).

Google Analytics and log analysis

Web analytics is generally focused on log analysis or page tagging. Log analysis makes use of the server logs from where the data is hosted to gain insights into the accessing of files that have been requested by a browser. Page tagging involves inserting a piece of JavaScript code within each web page so that a web analytics program is provided with the data. Page tagging analytics programs have user-friendly interfaces, with a focus on page views and tracking customer behaviour, and are now widely adopted; Google Analytics alone, the most widely adopted example of page tagging analytics, is now on 57.7% of all websites (W3Techs, 2013). Importantly page tagging allows for the investigation of web analytics even in instances where the site owner cannot access the server logs, for example when hosting a blog or website externally. As is noted throughout this book however, no web tool is perfect, and page tagging has its limitations. This is most noticeable with page tagging if users have JavaScript disabled in their browser, which makes a visitor appear invisible to the analytics program, or they have cookies disabled, which makes returning visitors appear as new visitors. Google also provides plug-ins that allow people to opt out of having their data collected by Google Analytics (https://tools.google.com/dlpage/gaoptout). Page tagging analytics would fail to alert an institution to inline linking of its images, the practice where HTML code is placed on one site that displays an image from another site.

As Google Analytics is the most popular form of internal web analytics a brief overview is provided to give an indication of the type of data that is available, although it should be noted that free alternatives are available. These include Piwik (http://piwik.org) and Open Web Analytics (www.openwebanalytics.com). These are likely to be of particular interest to large institutions that may otherwise need to subscribe to Google Analytics' premium service, although the 10 million page free limit a month is likely to be sufficient for most smaller institutions.

Once the Google Analytics account has been set up, and the JavaScript inserted in the relevant pages, librarians may look forward to gaining valuable insights into their user activity. However, the first-time user of Google Analytics may quickly feel overwhelmed by the amount of data that is available, and how finely it can be spliced. Broadly speaking, for every visit, data is captured about the visitor, the content they view, and the traffic source from which they come. Visitor data not only includes when they requested the page, but also from where in the world, the browser, operating system, even screen resolution and Flash version available. This allows for extremely specific reports and visualizations, far beyond what is useful for most individuals and organizations. For example, Figure 4.1 shows a breakdown of the 434 visitors my blog has had by people based in Cairo according to their screen resolution. As this accounts for a mere 0.18% of the total visits

	Town/City	Screen Resolution ⊗	Visits ▼ ↓	Visits
1.	■ Cairo	1024x768	150	34.56%
2.	■ Cairo	320x480	53	12.21%
3.	■ Cairo	1280x800	47	10.83%
4.	░ Cairo	1366x768	43	9.91%
5.	■ Cairo	800x600	20	4.61%
6.	▨ Cairo	1440x900	16	3.69%
7.	■ Cairo	1152x864	12	2.76%
8.	░ Cairo	1280x1024	11	2.53%
9.	▨ Cairo	768x1024	8	1.84%
10.	▨ Cairo	1600x900	5	1.15%

Figure 4.1 Number of visitors to blog.webometrics.org.uk from Cairo according to screen resolution [Google and the Google logo are registered trademarks of Google Inc., used with permission]

my blog has received, and my content is not particularly aimed at the Egyptian community, I am unlikely to spend much time analysing these specific details too closely, but as thousands of such tables are available within a few clicks the metrics can quickly become a distraction.

In most instances users find the overview level of the five standard reports sufficient; these are starting points for digging into the data, providing insights into the data from five different perspectives: audience, traffic sources, content, conversions and real-time activity. Selecting one of these reports provides the user with an overview of the main associated metrics and hyperlinks for digging further into the data. For example, selecting the audience report provides an over-view of the number of visits, unique visitors, page views, pages viewed per visit, average visit duration, bounce rate and percentage of new visits (see Figure 4.2), as well as the option for narrowing the data further according to the demo-graphics of the audience.

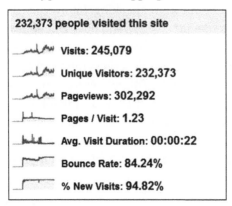

Figure 4.2
Overview of audience to Google Analytics
[Google and the Google logo are registered trademarks of Google Inc., used with permission]

Conversions enable the Google Analytics user to set specific goals that they want to achieve; for example a certain number of users, reaching a particular URL (or series of URLs), spending a certain amount of time on a visit, visiting a certain number of pages in a visit, or visiting an event (where additional code has been included to track interaction with website elements, e.g., Flash or AJAX elements).

As well as the standard reports, Google Analytics provides three additional methods of accessing the data simply:

- *dashboards* – allow summaries of the different reports to be displayed on one page
- *shortcuts* – the Google Analytic equivalent of bookmarks, allowing users to access the most specific of finds quickly
- *intelligence events* – enable automatic alerts for certain situations, e.g., a significant drop or rise in the number of page views or visits.

With so much data that can be viewed, it is important that librarians focus only on the most significant aspects and set up appropriate dashboards, shortcuts and intelligence events. The goals are likely to vary according to the type of library and the particular content within which the page tags have been placed. Public librarians inevitably pay particular attention to visits within the local area, while university librarians may be particularly interested in those accessing the website via the university network. Where a blog has been set up there may be particular interest in whether visitors go from their landing page to the blog's front page; where a tutorial has been placed online over many pages there is likely to be interest in whether the pages have all been viewed in order, or whether people have dropped out along the way.

Once appropriate metrics have been selected, and areas for improvement identified, it may be necessary to take appropriate action: where views are particularly low for one page it may be necessary to highlight the page more on other pages; where page views are low for the site overall it may be necessary to promote the site via social media or elsewhere; where visitors regularly break away from a series of pages at the same point, it may be necessary to see whether the page structure or content can be improved so people follow through with the series. In many instances the most appropriate action may be to do nothing. Librarians may spend a day trying to discover why the numbers have fallen in one particular area, only for them to have picked up the next day before there has been the opportunity to change anything. Features such as Google Analytics' real-time report, which provides live information about users currently on a site, encourage an obsession with the now, whereas in most instances librarians would be advised to look at longer term trends.

As a general rule people, whether library staff or library users, do not like to be measured, and steps should be taken to show them the benefits of any measurement that is proposed. This is particularly important with Google Analytics as it does not simply make use of data that already exists, but collects new data. The ability for users to opt out has always been recognized, and has recently been the subject of a European e-privacy directive, more commonly known as the Cookie law. At the time of writing (summer 2013) implied consent is considered sufficient by the Information Commissioner's Office in the UK (2012), which can be achieved by having an explicit privacy and cookie policy on a website. However, library professionals might want to go one step further and have an explicit acceptance of cookies before they start to collect data, although this will bias the data in favour of the sort of people who agree to accept cookies.

Although page tagging through a service such as Google Analytics is primarily for the purpose of web analytics, understanding the types of information that is available through such a service may also be useful for some webometric studies. Whereas the data collected from a single site is unlikely to be of use for many webometric studies, it could be that a webometric study makes use of the data from a host of websites through freedom of information requests.

Wikimetrics

Wikis, like blogs and other hosted content, may also make use of Google Analytics to evaluate a site's impact. After all, if no one is visiting a wiki that is aimed at the general public and takes a lot of staff hours to update, questions will inevitably be asked about whether it is a good use of resources. It is also of interest how people are contributing to a wiki, whether users are merely viewing content, or making efforts to contribute to pages. The ability to access this information varies according to the software, as well as the additional plug-ins, extensions and other software that have been built by the user community. For example, StatMediaWiki (http://statmediawiki. forja.rediris.es) allows for data about the number of edits that pages have received and users have made to be aggregated from across a wiki. Although the exact nature of this data varies according to the software, it may be broadly considered from the perspective of users and wiki pages. As always the exact metrics that are important depend on the purpose of the wiki.

Page-centric metrics generally provide information about the number of edits a page has received, the number of different editors who have edited a page, and how recently pages have been edited. The number of edits is generally an indication of interest in a subject, and a large number of edits is associated with a rise in the quality of the article. Where a topic has the potential to be particularly controversial, it may be that a large number of different editors are considered important, in an effort to provide balance.

User-centric metrics may provide information about the number of edits each user has made, and the number of pages they have edited. Where a wiki is not receiving as many contributions as had been anticipated, it is necessary to investigate who is making contributions. For example, although 250,000 new accounts are created for Wikipedia every month, only 300,000 users have made more than ten edits (Wikipedia, 2013c).

As with the implementation of Google Analytics on a website, librarians may want to identify goals and actions, but rather than tweaking web content themselves to increase traffic, they might attempt to find ways of increasing the contributions of editors. Although it may be that the best way to increase contributions is for librarians to lead by example, keeping a large wiki up to date may take considerable effort.

The topic of wikimetrics is revisited in Chapters 5 and 7, where wikimetrics for webometric, bibliometric and scientometric research are considered with reference to the special case of Wikipedia.

External metrics

This section looks at two principal types of source of information that may be used for external evaluative metrics: tools that provide insights into users' browsing behaviour, and tools that provide insights into the traces that are left online. In some cases the same tool may be used in both instances; for example Alexa, the web information service, provides information about user traffic and about a website's number of inlinks.

User behaviour

Increasingly there is a lot of online user behaviour that leaves explicit online traces. If someone uploads 50 of their holiday snaps to Flickr, then (unless they have implemented certain privacy settings) there will be 50 additional images that people can see online. However, much of user behaviour remains hidden. With the exception of some social media sites that explicitly promote the number of views or likes something has had, much of our online user activity remains hidden from the general public. Yet there are tools that can provide insights at an aggregated level, including those which give insights into web traffic and search behaviour.

Alexa

There are a number of online services that provide information about web traffic from across the web rather than a single site: Compete (www. compete.com), Quantcast (www.quantcast.com) and Alexa (www.alexa.com). Although each of these sites has premium accounts they also provide a certain amount of information for free, e.g., providing traffic information purely for the US. Nonetheless such sites can provide useful information for web analytical and webometric purposes.

The way each of the sites collects its data varies. For example, Quantcast provides a web analytics service, and collects anonymized data from those making use of the service (Quantcast, 2013); Compete's data is collected from a sample of 2 million US internet users (Compete, 2013); Alexa's data is collected from the Alexa toolbar users, with the data then normalized to correct for biases in the data sampling (Alexa, 2013a). Each of the sampling methods has its limitations: Quantcast's data is less reliable for those sites that are not using Quantcast analytics, Compete is very US-centric, and Alexa is inevitably biased in favour of the behaviour of those most likely to install the Alexa toolbar (web analysts and search engine optimizers) (see Figure 4.3). Nonetheless, as with so many web metrics, although they may not give definitive answers, these sites can nonetheless provide useful indicators, especially for the most popular websites where data is likely to be more accurate. Alexa provides free access to the widest range of data, with some additional data restricted to those who have installed the Alexa toolbar, and most appropriately for a book on web metrics aimed at librarians, is named after the Library of Alexandria (Quint, 1998). In 2013 automatic access to the data was available on a pay per use basis – $0.15 per 1000 requests.

Figure 4.3 The Alexa toolbar

Rather than providing absolute numbers of visitors, Alexa provides information about traffic rank – based on the number of page views and the number of users; reach percentage – the percentage of global internet users who visit a site; page view percentage – the estimated percentage of global page views on a particular site; page views per user – the estimated number of unique page views per user for a particular site; bounce – the proportion of visits that consist of a single page view; time on site – the estimated daily time spent on a page; and search percentage – the estimated percentage of daily visits that come from a search engine. Importantly, unlike log analysis and page tagging, comparisons may be made between websites, although there are limitations. For example, Alexa only allows data at the domain level, and the data is ranked rather than absolute, so there can be greater fluctuation further down and it is not possible to add data from multiple domains. These limitations can be seen when comparing data from the national libraries of the five biggest countries of the European Union.

It is easy to imagine librarians who are interested in comparing their library with similar institutions wanting to make use of Alexa for web analytic purposes. Table 4.1 shows the Alexa traffic rank and reach percentage for the national libraries of the five biggest countries in the European Union. While it clearly shows that the National Library of France has the most traffic, followed by the British Library, it is less clear about the positioning of the national libraries of Germany, Spain and Italy. The German National Library is ranked higher than the National Library of Spain (albeit not by much), but the positioning of the Italian national libraries is less clear.

Table 4.1 Alexa traffic rank of national libraries of five biggest EU members in March 2013

National Library	Alexa traffic rank	Reach percentage
German National Library (www.dnb.de)	94,258	0.00154%
National Library of France (www.bnf.fr)	15,272	0.0079%
British Library (www.bl.uk)	25,550	0.00566%
National Central Library of Rome (www.bncrm.librari.beniculturali.it)	45,084	0.00340%
National Central Library of Florence (www.bncf.firenze.sbn.it)	91,788	0.00142%
National Library of Spain (www.bne.es)	97,980	0.00137%

In the first instance Italy does not have one national library, but two, one in Florence and one in Rome, so a decision needs to be made whether to aggregate the data or not. Although the traffic rankings of two sites cannot be combined the reach percentage can, albeit not precisely as there may be a proportion of visitors who visited both sites and they will be counted twice. However, the bigger problem with identifying the traffic of the Italian national libraries is the fact that neither the National Central Library of Florence nor the National Central Library of Rome has its own domain name: the National Central Library of Florence uses a sub-domain of the National Library Service (www.sbn.it), and the National Central Library of Rome uses a sub-domain of the Italian Ministry of Culture (www.beniculturali.it). Alexa provides details of which sub-domains are visited by users, but does not provide a fine enough level of granularity for either of the Italian national libraries; although it is possible to discover that 17.21% of sbn.it visitors visit the firenze.sbn.it sub-domain information is not provided about the finer bncf.firenze.sbn.it domain. Equally, while it is possible to discover that 6.33% of beniculturali.it visitors visit the librari.beniculturali.it sub-domain, information is not provided about the finer bncrm.librari.beniculturali.it.

Limitations regarding the sub-domains and the limitations of the data collection methodology are likely to affect the insights Alexa can provide about many libraries; libraries are often part of larger organizations or entities and the traffic they receive is unlikely to be significant enough for Alexa to provide reliable results. Nevertheless where websites receive a significantly large amount of traffic, and have an appropriate URL, Alexa can provide insights that concur with our real-world experiences of rises and falls in traffic and the demographic information that Alexa provides about users.

Among the top-ranked websites we can see that although Google.com continues to be the top-ranked website overall, at weekends it is overtaken by Facebook, the social network site that has come to play such an important part in people's personal lives. In comparison LinkedIn, a more business orientated social network site, has its traffic rank fall at weekends, with its rank regularly falling from 10th to 16th. This is backed up by the demographic information for the two sites, which is based on the answers that are provided to a short questionnaire when people install the Alexa toolbar. LinkedIn is overly represented by people at work rather than home. LinkedIn can also be seen to have an older and more educated audience, albeit not as old, educated or poor as the audience of the national libraries. As well as providing insights into age, education, income and browsing location (e.g., work or home) Alexa also provides insights into a website audience's gender, income, ethnicity and whether or not they have children, and which countries visitors are visiting the sites from. In the data for national library sites language and historical connections are reflected: the British Library gets a lot of traffic from the US and India; the National Library of France gets a lot of traffic from Algeria; and the German National Library gets a lot of traffic from Austria. It is important to remember, however, that as we look at a finer level of granularity that there is more room for error as the data is based on fewer individuals. Although we can provide logical reasons for the British Library getting traffic from the US and India, that it also gets a similar amount of traffic from Thailand as India, and less from Canada than the Netherlands, may be more surprising.

Alexa provides a number of ways of identifying sites for investigation. As well as a search facility allowing for the entering of keywords (or URLs if a site of interest is already known) Alexa enables the browsing of the top 500 websites globally and for each country, as well as the browsing of websites by category (e.g., the top library websites www.alexa.com/topsites/category/ Reference/Libraries), although as the directory is created automatically caution should be taken before taking any categorization as the basis for a web metric investigation. Alexa also provides a CSV file of the top 1 million globally ranked websites, which is updated daily for anyone who wants a more extensive view of the rankings.

Alexa's use of sub-domains and the restricted number of users who have installed the toolbar may limit its use to web analytics to larger websites, but it has been used for a number of studies, including a comparison of Chinese recruitment websites (Zhan and Yan, 2011), Chinese and US social network sites (Li, 2011) and Malaysian universities (Didegah and Erfanmanesh, 2010). Alexa has also been used as a method of sampling the most popular sites in a particular area for further investigation (e.g., Price and Grann, 2012). More innovatively it has been used as a basis for investigations into the linguistic characteristics of domain names (Xiang, 2012), and into the impact linking has on a website's traffic by comparing Alexa traffic information with the link information (Ennew et al., 2005), a topic that is returned to below in the section 'User traces'.

An ever more important limitation of Alexa for providing insights into web traffic data is that it is heavily linked to the browser toolbar, and as users increasingly use mobile devices to access content it may become less relevant, especially in comparison with a tool that is platform neutral, for example Google.

Google Trends

Google is the number one ranked traffic destination according to Alexa (at least for five days of the week), and the millions of people entering their queries provide a huge potential resource for people interested in users' online behaviour. The potential interest of users' online searches to online marketers and researchers has been recognized for a number of years, although search engines are more careful these days in taking precautions to protect users' privacy. In 2006 AOL Research released search log data for a random sample of 658,000 users that was 'anonymized' by providing identification numbers rather than usernames or IP (internet protocol) addresses. Unfortunately many people's searches contain identifiable pieces of information: we search for ourselves, our home towns, and the places where we work. This means that 'anonymized' data can nonetheless lead to people being identified if multiple searches by the same user are grouped together. Lessons have been learnt, and now services are more careful about protecting users' privacy and aggregating individuals.

Google Trends (www.google.com/trends) provides insights into the search terms that have been entered into one of five Google products: web search, image search, news search, product search and YouTube search. On visiting

Google Trends the user is prompted to enter one or more comma-separated search terms. The default is then to display worldwide interest in these search terms in a graph covering searches from January 2004 until the present day (see Figure 4.4). The total number of searches is not displayed on the graphs, but rather the number of times a search is requested is normalized according to the total number of searches, and then presented on a graph from 0 to 100. This information can also be downloaded in CSV format, which can in turn be loaded into a spreadsheet or a text editor.

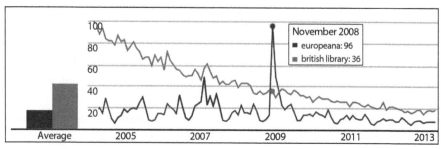

Figure 4.4 Google Trends for searches for the terms Europeana and British Library [Google and the Google logo are registered trademarks of Google Inc., used with permission]

The data can not only be limited to different places and different time periods, but location and time can also form the starting point for interrogating the search data. For example, finding the top and rising search terms at a particular time or in a specific country.

It may be argued that search results are interesting because they reflect actions rather than words (Dzielinski, 2012), and the two are not always the same thing. Although one may expect a large time-consuming and expensive survey of the general British public to find that they consider the British Library to be a good thing, worthy of public funding, Figure 4.4 suggests that interest in the British Library is falling. There are alternative explanations for the reduction in the number of searches for the British Library between 2004 and 2013; for example, an increasing number of people are visiting the site directly rather than having to search for it; the British Library's content is shared so seamlessly on other sites that no one needs to go searching for it; or there is a limitation of the tool itself (for example, Hubbard (2011) notes a 'decay rate' for a number of common English words). Without a clear reason, though, the reduction in the number of people visiting the site would definitely seem to be something worthy of further investigation.

Since search data was first found to be an early indicator of flu levels (Eysenbach,2006) and the unemployment rate (Ettredge, Gerdes and Karuga,

2005) there have been an increasing number of studies making use of search query data for economics and public health investigations, many of which have made use of the data that is easily available through Google Trends.

Recent economic studies have found the following: an increase in searches related to the economy reflected an increase in economic uncertainty (Dzielinski, 2012); internet users from countries with a higher GDP are more likely to search for information about the future than the past (Pries et al., 2012); and search data can be used to provide a wide range of economic indicators about consumption (Vosen and Schmidt, 2012) and consumer confidence (Choi and Varian, 2012).

While Eysenbach (2006) showed the potential of search queries for epidemiological investigations, interest gained momentum following the release of Google Flu Trends (www.google.org/flutrends/) and the publication of an associated article in *Nature* (Ginsberg et al., 2009). Google Flu Trends aggregates search terms that have been found to correlate with cycles of influenza so that earlier indications of flu epidemics can be provided through the accumulation of information from health care professionals. As later studies have shown, Google Flu Trends does not necessarily indicate flu, but rather the spread of flu-like symptoms (Ortiz et al., 2010), and recent seasonal flu epidemics have found discrepancies with the levels indicated by Google Flu Trends (Butler, 2013), which may be attributable to feedback in the system (when Google Flu reports high flu searches news organizations report it and people start searching with flu related search terms). Nevertheless the potential of search terms to provide indicators of infectious diseases is of growing interest. Seifter et al. (2010) have suggested that the method may be applied more widely, showing how searches for seasonal diseases such as Lyme disease correlate appropriately, while the Google Flu Trends website has been extended to include information about the activity of dengue fever, which can be indicated far earlier with search data than traditional sources (Chan et al., 2011).

Using Google Trends for information about public health is not restricted to providing information on communicable diseases: Walcott et al. (2011) have shown that search data correlates with stroke prevalence in the 50 US states; Schuster, Rogers and McMahon (2010) found that search engine queries for medical information correlate with pharmaceutical revenue and overall health care utilization in a community. Search data also provides a way of investigating the impact of health information campaigns, which may not have a single destination site. For example, Glynn et al. (2011) identified increased search activity for breast cancer correlating with breast cancer awareness campaigns.

The potential of search data is not limited to macroeconomic indicators or public health information. Other studies have identified the potential of search data for forecasting cinema admissions (Hand and Judge, 2012) and trends in vehicle shopping interest (Du and Kamakura, 2012). Librarians can use search data to provide insights into their organization's online presence, and to gauge any change in interest in different subjects, emerging technologies, and even continuing interest in books over time (a topic that is returned to in Chapter 7). It is still early days, and the potential of search data has only relatively recently been recognized; there is still much work to do in finding out what can and cannot be predicted, and the appropriateness of particular terms. Search queries that one may expect to correlate with a particular activity are not always found to do so. For example, while it may be expected that there is a correlation between the number of searches around the topic of suicide and the actual number of suicides, no correlation was found when a comparison was made with official government statistics in Japan (Sueki, 2011). The ability to interrogate search data in the future successfully will also be heavily dependent on the tools that are available, and in 2011 Google released a new tool, Google Correlate (www.google.com/trends/correlate), which enables the identification of queries with a similar pattern to a particular data series.

User traces

While tools such as Alexa and Google Trends provide insights into the public's online behaviour, an additional source for indicators of the public's thoughts and feelings is the content of the web itself. Individuals and organizations of all shapes and sizes and across every discipline now consider a web presence essential. Whereas once the costs and technical knowledge necessary for publishing content may have excluded great swathes of the public from publishing their own content, so-called Web 2.0 technologies have enabled billions of people to publish content online. The biggest social network sites now have hundreds of millions of users publishing content on their sites, and the biggest of these are discussed in more detail in Chapter 5. It is important to recognize, however, that there is a far wider range of content that is published on the web than is published on the dominant social network sites, although capturing the data creates its own set of difficulties.

Most evaluative webometric investigations that have made use of users' online traces may be broadly categorized as link analyses. Since it was first proposed that search engine data could be used to calculate a web impact factor for aggregations of web pages (e.g., a country or website), hyperlinks have formed the basis of many evaluative investigations. Although as was discussed in Chapter 3, the changing nature of the tools that are available means that the hyperlink is not the only online trace that is used as a measure of impact.

Hyperlinks: Alexa, search engine optimizers and web crawlers

Although hyperlinks are more difficult to identify these days than when link information was widely available through search engines, they can nonetheless still be identified.

Alexa.com provides information about web traffic and the number of sites it has identified linking to a particular domain. It not only states the number of sites it has identified linking to a particular domain, but also shows the top 100 sites linking to a particular domain. Alexa's 'sites linking in' has now been proposed as an alternative data source for web hyperlink analysis (Vaughan, 2012), and has been used to compare keyword analysis with link analysis (Vaughan and Romero-Frías, 2012).

There are, however, a number of limitations with Alexa as a data source about web links. As with web traffic data, information is only available at the domain level – it is possible to see the number of sites that link to a university website (e.g., www.wlv.ac.uk) but not the number of sites linking to a particular sub-domain or directory (e.g., cybermetrics.wlv.ac.uk). Alexa also only counts the number of sites linking in (operationalized according to a web URL), which means that it is not possible to use alternative aggregations such as web pages or directories linking in. It also only lists the top 100 sites, and only one link is shown per site, so only an extremely limited content analysis may take place to determine why links are placed to a website.

Nevertheless, it is possible to see how Alexa's 'sites linking in' data may form the basis of evaluative webometric and web analytic investigations for librarians. Table 4.2 (overleaf) shows the number of sites linking in for the Russell Group of UK universities (www.russellgroup.ac.uk). Despite being a relatively homogenous set of universities, lacking the real diversity of UK higher educational institutions, the number of sites linking in to each university domain is found to correlate negatively with a university's ranking according to the *Guardian* (2012) (statistically significant at the 5% level using Spearman's rank). While being statistically significant at the 5% level is unlikely to see the dismissal of existing university rankings, it nonetheless provides a useful additional source of information as an indicator not only of

University	URL	Alexa ranking	*Guardian* university 'sites linking in'
University of Birmingham	www.birmingham.ac.uk/	30	2062
University of Bristol	www.bristol.ac.uk/	18	4299
University of Cambridge	www.cam.ac.uk/	1	42,574
Cardiff University	www.cardiff.ac.uk/	40	9102
Durham University	www.dur.ac.uk/	7	9902
University of Edinburgh	www.ed.ac.uk/home	15	23,933
University of Exeter	www.ex.ac.uk/	10	10,590
University of Glasgow	www.gla.ac.uk/	14	15,708
Imperial College London	www3.imperial.ac.uk/	13	6993
King's College London	www.kcl.ac.uk/	31	8865
University of Leeds	www.leeds.ac.uk/	37	14,843
University of Liverpool	www.liv.ac.uk/	45	7789
London School of Economics & Political Science	www.lse.ac.uk/	3	13,197
University of Manchester	www.manchester.ac.uk/	41	18,002
Newcastle University	www.ncl.ac.uk/	33	12,853
University of Nottingham	www.nottingham.ac.uk/	26	11,787
University of Oxford	www.ox.ac.uk/	2	43,774
Queen Mary, University of London	www.qmul.ac.uk/	36	7629
Queen's University Belfast	www.qub.ac.uk/	53	5646
University of Sheffield	www.sheffield.ac.uk/	42	2292
University of Southampton	www.soton.ac.uk/	22	13,348
University College London	www.ucl.ac.uk/	6	23,484
University of Warwick	www2.warwick.ac.uk/	5	11,927
University of York	www.york.ac.uk/	17	9699

Table 4.2 Alexa 'sites linking in' of UK universities in March 2013

ranking but also of web presence and visibility. Presence and visibility are important from a web analytics perspective, providing insights into the impact web content is having, irrespective of whether such impact can be seen as an indicator of an institution's ranking.

Alexa is not the only source of information about inlinks. Webometrics.info, which provides a presence and visibility ranking for 21,250 higher education institutions (something that would have been prohibitively expensive by traditional means), uses data collected from ahrefs (http://ahrefs.com) and Majestic SEO (www.majesticseo.com). These tools are primarily designed for search engine optimization specialists, people who try to improve the ranking of other people's websites, although they can also be of use to researchers. For example, in their analysis of the relationship between the expenditure of US academic libraries and their web presence, Orduña-Malea and Regazzi (2013) collected inlink data from Majestic SEO and the similar service Open Site Explorer (www.opensiteexplorer.org). Unlike Alexa.com these services enable the investigation of linking to sub-domains as well as domains, a crucial aspect in Orduña-Malea and Regazzi's (2013) investigation as the library websites and services made use of a wide range of sub-domains and directories. The full data from each of these sites is only available with a subscription.

Alternative links: URL citations and web mentions

As was mentioned in Chapter 3, although none of the major search engines explicitly provide link search functionality, and only Bing provides a suitable API, search engines may still be used to provide insights through the appearance of web mentions of an organizational name or URL citations (where the URL itself is visible, rather than some other text being hyperlinked to a particular URL).

If all that is required is an estimated number of URL citations or web mentions for a set of websites, unless it is an excessively large number of queries, it would be possible to enter the queries by hand.

For a large number of queries, or if a researcher wants to analyse the page's URL citing a site or mentioning a particular term, automating the process is preferable. This may be done by either writing a program to make use of the Bing API or, the easier option, making use of Webometric Analyst (http://lexiurl.wlv.ac.uk) from the Statistical Cybermetrics Research Group. Webometric Analyst is discussed in more detail in Chapters 5 and 6, where it is used for the analysis of YouTube comments and a relational link analysis.

Search engine rankings

It would be remiss to leave a discussion revolving around the impact of websites without addressing the elephant in the web metrics room: search engine ranking. Search engines play a crucial role in helping people find information online today; if it cannot be found from entering a few carefully chosen keywords, it may as well not exist for many users. Crucially, it is not enough that the search engine finds a relevant document; it must rank the documents in such a fashion that those that are most likely to meet a user's requirements are ranked not only on the first page, but at the top of the first page. Google famously started on its journey to search engine dominance by making use of the PageRank algorithm, which took into consideration the link structure of the web, not only accounting for the number of links that a website received, but also weighting each of those links according to how many links they received in turn (Brin and Page, 1998). This is now only one of many different signals Google uses to rank its content, and these days a whole search engine optimization industry revolves around trying to identify and manipulate these signals so that people can get their pages to the top of the search engine rankings. With such a manipulated marketplace, can search engine rankings provide a meaningful indicator of impact?

The potential manipulation of the marketplace has an impact on not only a search engine's ranking, but also other web metrics, such as the number of links that a website has pointing to it. The difference is that the number of web links may be seen, and the reasons they are placed investigated. In comparison, Google's ranking algorithm is kept hidden, although people regularly take steps to reverse engineer it. While the PageRank part of the ranking algorithm is known and easily accessible through multiple tools and sites (e.g., www.prchecker.info), only a single number is provided on a scale of 0 to 10, providing little room for comparison between similar websites. As an alternative, in the evaluation of the impact of US academic library websites Orduña-Malea and Regazzi (2013) make use of a similar impact measure, the Domain MozRank from Open Site Explorer (www.opensiteexplorer.org), which is on a scale of 1 to 100.

As search engines attempt to outmanoeuvre search engine optimizers and improve user experience, one of the results will be increased personalization, with different users receiving a different search engine ranking. The idea of search engine ranking as an indicator of impact will be increasingly meaningless.

Web metrics should be based on open criteria, so they may be verified or challenged as necessary, not criteria that are hidden for the sake of commercial advantage. A high or low ranking on Google may indeed be a reflection of a site's quality, but it could just as easily be a reflection of a quirk of the algorithm. It is also important that metrics can be validated, so that the reasons links are placed and mentions are made can be explored. This may be achieved through sentiment and content analysis.

Sub-sections of the web

Where detailed information about the impact of a website or domain is required, it may be that a web crawler is more appropriate. The SocSciBot web crawler (http://socscibot.wlv.ac.uk) was specifically designed for link analysis research, and has formed the basis of many investigations. Although they were briefly usurped by the search engine APIs, they have always been more appropriate for certain webometric studies, for example, where the interlinking between a small number of known websites was being investigated, and the researcher wanted to be sure that the sites had been fully indexed. The Internet Archive also has an open source crawler available, Heritrix (http://crawler.archive.org). This is primarily designed for archival purposes rather than for link analysis, but as it is open source those with the requisite programming skills can adapt it to their needs. The Internet Archive has also offered access to one of their crawls of the web, 80 terabytes of information from 2.7 billion URLs for those who are interested in analysing a large section of the web (Internet Archive, 2012). Common Crawl (http://commoncrawl.org) also provides access to web crawl data, which can be accessed and analysed by anyone.

In many instances, however, the additional work necessary to make use of crawl data may be of little additional value, and librarians' time may be better spent using alternative types of information.

Although the depreciation of the major search engines' link functionality, and the restriction of their APIs, has made it increasingly difficult to gather insights into the linking to a website from across the web, it is nonetheless possible to understand the impact of a website within sub-sections of the web. The vast size of social networking sites means that they can be an important source of information, for example, how many times has a website been mentioned on Twitter or on Google Plus, or how many times has a site been bookmarked on Delicious or dug on Digg. Some of this type of information is included in some SEO link services (e.g., http://ahrefs.com), some in more specialized tools (e.g., http://topsy.com), and in some instances it may be gathered from the sites themselves (e.g., http://delicious.com). There will be a more detailed discussion of analysing data from social network sites in the next chapter.

A systematic approach to content analysis

As has already been mentioned 'raw data only tells half the story' (Marek, 2011, 6) and if insights are going to be supported it is important that steps are taken to determine the reasons why links have been placed. As was mentioned in Chapter 2, where a large quantity of structured data needs to be analysed then a sentiment analysis may be appropriate (and this is discussed in more detail in the next chapter), but for the broad range of content that may be found linking or mentioning a website a content analysis is likely to be more appropriate.

A web metric content analysis is a systematic approach to analysing the reasons for content creation through human inspection of the content and, where necessary, the surrounding content. A content analysis may be used to determine type of author of content (e.g., public or private, research group, academic department or support services), the nature of particular content (e.g., what is contained within an image), the reason why a link was made (e.g., to express a relationship with the linked website or merely a useful resource), or the reason a certain phrase was mentioned (e.g., to express displeasure with a company or to highlight good practice). A wide range of content has been the focus of content analysis: inlinks to business websites (Vaughan, Gao and Kipp, 2006); outlinks on academic websites (Stuart, Thelwall and Harries, 2007), restaurant reviews (Pantelidis, 2010), the expressions of politicians in images (Ozel and Park, 2012) and HPV vaccine information (Madden et al., 2012). In each case a systematic approach has been taken to investigating the nature of the content.

The content analysis methodology is broadly formed of five stages:

- identify question(s) to be answered
- select a sample of content
- develop an appropriate classification scheme
- classify content
- analyse findings.

Identify question(s) to be answered

As can be seen from the examples of content analysis discussed above, the range of questions that could form the basis of a content analysis are limited only by the imagination of the researcher. A web analytic investigation might investigate the reasons links have been placed to their own and competitor websites, while a scientometric study might investigate research areas of interest associated with a particular discipline. Without a clear question it is impossible to take an appropriate data sample or develop an appropriate classification scheme.

Select sample of content

How a sample of websites is selected depends heavily on the tools that are being used to collect data. If a web crawler has been used to collect data, there may be many thousands of potential results for classification; if data has been collected from a search engine there will only be up to 1000 results; if the content analysis is on comments about an organization, there may only be a handful. As the appearance of many web phenomena follows a power-law distribution (e.g., the vast majority of links will occur on a handful of sites), it is important to take steps to account for this.

For example, imagine that a webometric researcher is interested in the reasons universities are linking to items in the arXiv.org e-print repository; whether the links are synonymous with traditional citations, or on researchers' home pages highlighting their own papers. A crawl of the UK academic web space might identify 83,000 pages with links to the archive, far too many for the researcher to classify all of them by hand, so they decide to take a sample of 500. However, merely taking a random sample of 500 URLs from the 83,000 will inadvertently weight the conclusions in line with those institutions that have an abnormally large number of links. For example, Southampton University hosts a mirror of the arXiv.org at xxx.soton.ac.uk. In the same way as it is appropriate to count links at the domain level, it might be better to take a random sample of 50 URLs from each of the 100 or so academic domains linking to arXiv.org, and then take a random sample from this smaller set.

Although the full set of results may be available if the data has been collected by a web crawler, search engines typically restrict users to the first 1000 results. Webometric Analyst (http://lexiurl.wlv.ac.uk) allows for the downloading of the results from Bing, though if the researcher wants to take the results from Google the results need to be scraped from the HTML pages. Although results can be downloaded in a CSV file format with the toolbar plug-in SEOQuake (www.seoquake.com), precautions should be taken so that too many queries are not sent to Google at once, as Google may then ban the IP address for a number of hours. To get the most representative sample of results, it is important to turn off personal results, and if the site Google.com keeps redirecting the searcher to a local variation (e.g., Google.co.uk) then www.google.com/ncr is a link from which Google will not redirect.

Develop an appropriate classification scheme

It is important that the classification scheme(s) should reflect the question(s) that is (are) the focus of the content analysis, and that the categories are as distinct and clear as possible. For example, returning to the above example of the webometric researcher who is interested in the reasons universities are linking to items in the arXiv.org e-print repository, the researcher may decide that the question should be approached in two parts: who is linking from universities to arXiv.org, and the reason for link placement, and that a separate classification scheme should be developed for each.

There are two main approaches that can be taken to the development of the scheme: an iterative approach or post-coordinate clustering. An iterative scheme is developed during the process of content analysis, with new categories being created as necessary. Post-coordinate clustering is more suitable where more than one classifier is being used, and involves visiting a random selection of content and then devising appropriate categories for content that seems to be similar. Post-coordinate clustering also allows for the development of a classification protocol, an explicit statement of the categories and the content included, to help with consistency and inter-classifier agreement.

Classify content

Classification is rarely a black and white process. In even the most well designed classification scheme there can be subjects that seem to straddle multiple categories, or where the content is ambiguous (e.g., is a comment serious or sarcastic?). In such situations a classification protocol helps to explain to interested parties how the classification scheme has been applied.

Depending on the purpose of the analysis it may be that multiple classifiers are necessary. A preliminary study for internal purposes may require only a single classifier; for more extensive studies that may impact policy decisions, more than one classifier may be necessary. Where more than one classifier is used the second classifier may classify a proportion of the links that have already been classified by a first classifier (e.g., 10%), and then inter-classifier consistency may be tested using a statistical test such as Krippendorff's alpha (Krippendorff, 2012).

If there are large discrepancies it may be necessary to return to step three, and repeat the process with a more explicit classification protocol, or to have a coarser grained categorization.

Analyse findings

The final step is drawing conclusions from the findings. For a small-scale analysis of comments about a library it may be enough to leave it as '6 comments were positive, and 3 were negative', but if a more extensive test has taken place it may be necessary to apply additional statistical tests.

For example, webometric researchers interested in the reasons universities are linking to items in the arXiv.org e-print repository may want to determine whether the difference in the reasons for link placement on different types of pages is statistically significant, in which case the chi-square test would be suitable.

Conclusion

This chapter has discussed a wide range of internal and external tools and approaches for evaluating the impact of web content. Even for something as simple as measuring the impact of a website, a battery of metrics may be easily provided from a wide variety of sources. A few of those mentioned above include:

- page views (Google Analytics)
- bounce rate (Google Analytics)
- traffic rank (Alexa)
- sites linking in (Alexa)
- inlinks (www.majesticseo.com)
- URL citations (Bing)
- PageRank (Google)
- Domain MozRank (www.opensiteexplorer.org)
- number of bookmarks (http://delicious.com)
- number of tweeted links (http://topsy.com).

An exhaustive list would be seemingly without end, as the data may be endlessly spliced to provide finer grains of granularity (e.g., page views in Afghanistan or inlinking sites with positive comments). The most appropriate set of metrics depends on the purpose of the investigation and inevitably involves an element of trial and error.

Although web metrics have obvious potential for web analytic purposes, it should also be clear that the web has the potential to provide a far wider range of insights into real-world behaviour. While the web is increasingly being investigated for the provision of health and economic insights, it would seem as though the nature of such investigations is only limited to the imagination of the researcher and the tools that are available.

5

Evaluating social media impact

Introduction

Much of the information that is placed online is not on an individual's or an institution's personal server, but rather makes use of external sites and services: images are uploaded to Flickr; videos to YouTube; presentations to SlideShare; and comments to Twitter. Such sites and services not only ease the publishing process for individuals, but also enable the delivery of content that has the potential to go viral. There are advantages and disadvantages for web metrics. On the one hand external sites and services can provide additional or more complete metrics: they provide a large amount of data structured in the same manner, and it is theoretically possible for all data that meets a particular criterion to be retrieved. On the other hand metrics are severely limited to the functionality that the service allows; although the data may be structured, the website may not facilitate access to this data.

With such a wide range of services available, from a web analytic point of view it is necessary for librarians to ask which services are worthwhile (Vucovich et al., 2013), and at what point to stop spending the time and effort on a service. As with the web metrics discussed in the previous chapter, social media metrics offer the potential for a far wider range of insights than those into a library's own web presence. A handful of individual sites and services with hundreds of millions of users can also provide insights into a range of real-world user behaviour, forming the basis of a wide range of webometric investigations.

This chapter starts by considering the types of social network site that are available and the types of social network site content that librarians may be interested in evaluating. This is followed by a closer look at some of the popular social network sites that may form the basis of a web metric investigation, previous investigations that have taken place, and some of the tools that are available.

Aspects of social network sites

The web is dominated by a small number of sites, many of which have incorporated some level of social networking functionality. Boyd and Ellison's (2007) definition of a social network site comprises three parts, allowing users to construct a public profile in a bounded system, articulate connections to other users, and navigate the connections they and others make. This definition includes sites such as Facebook and Twitter, and sites which may not be primarily thought of as social networking sites, such as eBay and Wikipedia.

At the time of writing the list of social network sites on Wikipedia (2013a) included 200 'major active' social network sites, and a work that attempted to discuss metrics for each of them would become repetitive and quickly dated as the different social networking sites rise and fall, and the functionality changes. Some of these sites and services provide extensive APIs that enable a wide range of metrics to be calculated; others show extremely limited content. This chapter starts with the data that a web metrics researcher would wish to investigate if the data was available.

Boyd and Ellison's (2007) definition of a social network site comprises three parts, the public profile, the connections to other users, and the ability to navigate these connections, and each of these may form the basis of web metric investigations.

Profiles

When discussing profiles on social network sites it is useful to distinguish between the core portions of a profile which have a degree of permanence and the transitory aspects of the profile which may change regularly. For example, a Twitter user's core profile consists of a photo, their username, name, location, website and a biography of up to 160 characters. Although each of these may be changed by the user, they generally remain the same from day to day. The Twitter user's transient profile primarily consists of the updates that the user posts, as well as other people's updates that a user has categorized as 'favourites'. This content may be permanently available, but it is pushed away from the front of the profile as new content is created. The profile that a user can create on a social network site varies considerably according to the particular site, as well as over the lifetime of a service as functionality is added or discarded. The nature of the transient profile content is often the most obvious difference between social network sites: Twitter is primarily focused on short text-based updates (although it also allows additional content types); SlideShare is for presentations; and YouTube is for videos. Many of the sites also allow for an element of content creation on other people's transient profile space, e.g., leaving a message on another user's Facebook wall, or comment on another user's YouTube video. The core profiles also differ considerably, for example whereas Twitter's biography is an unstructured 160 characters of text, LinkedIn enables a far more structured biography about experience, education and skills, more in keeping with its role as a social network site for business professionals.

Depending on the accessibility of the information, any of the aspects of a profile may form the basis of a web metric investigation. There are many instances where a researcher may be interested in the demographics of a site's users or particular sub-set of users as expressed in the core profile: librarians contemplating making use of a social network site might wish to determine whether current members are those they wish to be interacting with; public librarians may collect data about the users in a local area (or who have expressed a relationship with a library) so they can ensure that the library meets the community's interest in different subjects; managers of commercial organizations may want to understand the demographics of those who express an interest in their products; managers of companies wishing to compete more effectively with their more successful competitors may wish to gather information on the skills of their competitors' staff to identify gaps in their areas of expertise.

Much of the web metric research focuses on the transient profile. This provides the opportunity to gain insights into people's perceptions of the world today, rather than when they created their profile: the number of positive comments a product has received in the last month is likely to provide greater insights into how it is perceived than a profile's likes and dislikes that may have been created years before. As with users' search behaviour, as exhibited through Google Trends (see Chapter 4), analysis of a large amount of transient profile information provides the opportunity to provide indicators for areas such as health and wellbeing and the economy. Unsurprisingly the focus of much of the research is on content that is text based, as opposed to videos and images, as this has the potential to be analysed automatically, or at least semi-automatically. Nevertheless there is also the potential for richer forms of content to be the focus of analyses, e.g., the topic of photos or videos that are being tagged or associated with a particular product or company.

Connections

The connections between profiles are often the focus of web metrics for web analytic purposes. The information is often immediately available and prominently displayed, whether the number of followers on Twitter, number of friends on Facebook, or subscribers on YouTube. It is important to recognize, however, that the nature of the relationship may differ considerably from that implied by the term assigned by the site: Facebook friends differ considerably from real-world friends; following on Twitter does not imply any agreement with the followee's opinions; and a YouTube subscriber does not necessarily value a subscription enough to part with money for it.

Although it may be in the interests of the social network sites that users spend time building their number of connections, and it could be argued that the prominence often given to the numbers builds in an element of competition, it is important that the value of the connections is kept in perspective, especially as the number of connections received may reflect a variety of behaviours besides the perceived quality of a user's account.

The importance of questioning a particular metric is best illustrated with a simple example: the number of followers of a Twitter account as an indicator of the success of the Twitter account. The simplest measure of impact for a library's Twitter account is its number of followers. Compare the number of followers for the Twitter accounts of two libraries and you could theoretically identify the library that was more successful on Twitter. For example, the Twitter account of University of Southampton Library (@UniSotonLibrary) has 484 followers, while the University of East Anglia Library (@UEALibrary) has 897 followers, seemingly indicating that the UEA's Twitter account is more successful. Unfortunately there are many different factors that may impact the number of followers an account has, both online and offline.

It would seem likely that the factors that influence the number of followers an account has include the number of accounts the account is following (Figure 5.1), and the number of updates that have been sent (Figure 5.2).

Figures 5.1 and 5.2 both have statistically significant positive correlations (significant at the 5% level using the Pearson correlation test), despite the more obvious outliers. For example, the fact that Bodleian Library has over 11,000 followers, despite following only 126 Twitter streams and updating the account an average of 1297 times, may be attributable to it being a library known worldwide, rather than anything intrinsic to the Twitter account.

A multiple regression analysis based on the data from these accounts (excluding the Bodleian Library) produces the following equation:

Expected followers = 1.08 × following + 1.85 × status updates

Such an equation allows the comparison of accounts that have been posting for different lengths of time and are following a different number of people. In fact using this formula we find that although the UEA Library has more followers, the University of Southampton Library may be considered to have

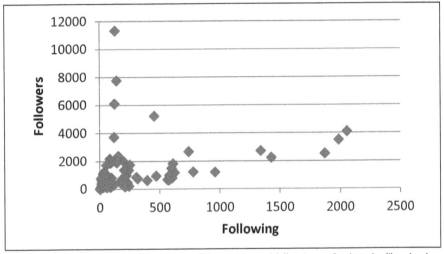

Figure 5.1 The number of followers and the number of followings of university libraries in the UK (April 2013)

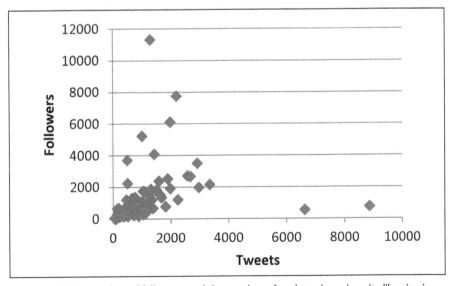

Figure 5.2 The number of followers and the number of updates by university libraries in the UK (April 2013)

the more successful online presence. While the UEA Library has only 80% of the expected number of followers, the University of Southampton Library has 38% more followers than expected! The factors that are considered in such an analysis do not have to be restricted to online information, but could include other publicly available information such as the university's number of students or library budget. The point is not that a library should not use the number of Twitter followers as an indicator (although it seems a bit too crude) or that it should consider numerous real-world factors (which seems excessive), but rather the importance of questioning metrics and recognizing their limitations.

Although a simple comparison of the number of connections is filled with pitfalls when it comes to measuring the impact of a profile, that does not mean that the direct connections cannot provide useful insights into the relationships between different actors, especially where different types of relationship are expressed, for example, through the use of lists on Twitter (where a user groups the people they are following together according to a category of their choice) or endorsements on LinkedIn (where a user endorses a particular skill of a contact). There are also a wide variety of indirect connections: users may have friends in common, share similar interests, have attended the same institution or have been members of the same organization.

The potential for connections to provide more than evaluative metrics, but rather form the basis of relational investigations is returned to in Chapter 6.

The ability to navigate: content views

The ability to navigate connections between profiles and view another person's content is an important aspect of engagement on social network sites: content is created to be seen. In some instances hard data is available about whether the content was viewed, in other cases it is necessary to rely on substitutes.

Although services like YouTube and SlideShare provide data about the number of views content has received, in the case of a status update on Twitter or Facebook there is no way of discerning how many people saw a comment. It may be that an update was posted at a time when all of a person's friends or followers were on the commute home, and by the time they logged on again one person's content had been superseded by that of other people. It is therefore often necessary to rely on approximate indicators for how often a particular piece of content has been seen. While this may not be ideal, they nonetheless may have the advantage of providing an indicator of what people thought of the content.

The number of connections that a user has may be the most accessible indicator of how many people have seen some content. Although while it may be expected that there would be a correlation between the number of connections and the number of views, depending on the type of content and the reason for the connection, the number of views for any single piece of content may be a very small proportion of the total number of connections. This can be seen most clearly on a social network site like YouTube, where the number of both connections and views that videos have received are clearly visible. A channel like 4oD Comedy, one of a number of YouTube channels from the UK television corporation Channel 4, has 125,473 subscribers at the time of writing, but many of the uploaded videos have had only hundreds of views months later.

The number of connections also fails to take into consideration the viral potential that is built into many social network sites. Someone on YouTube may only have a handful of subscribers, but because they upload a video that is of wide interest it may be viewed and shared many times; it is not unusual for people with dozens of subscribers to have a video that has been viewed millions of times. It may be that a better indication of the number of times content has been viewed is the number of times that other users have engaged with it. This may be replies or retweets on Twitter, likes on Facebook, or comments on most social network sites. Each can only be a rough indicator of the number of times a piece of content has been viewed, and absolute numbers are preferable, although it may not always be clear how the views are calculated.

Understanding how content has been viewed and responded to has obvious implications from the perspective of librarians publishing their own content. It is important that librarians understand whether the instruction videos are being used, whether the uploaded images are of interest to their user community, or whether the comments are deemed informative. Statistics about content views may also form the basis of webometric, bibliometric or scientometric studies: what content are people particularly interested in? What insights can it provide about real-world behaviour?

Typology of social network sites

Profile content, connections and content views may all form the basis of metrics, although as there is such a large and diverse selection of social network sites available it is useful to consider the types of metrics that may be of interest to librarians according to the uses to which a social network site is put in addition to the types of thing that may be measured.

Thelwall and Stuart (2010) identify three types of social network sites: socializing, networking and navigating sites. Socializing social network sites are those sites that support informal social communication, including sites like Facebook and Twitter, and align with most people's idea of a social network site. Networking social network sites are those designed for more formal interpersonal communication, such as the business social network site LinkedIn or the academic social network site ResearchGate (www. researchgate.net). Navigation social network sites are those sites which support the discovery of content through social network connections. They include YouTube for videos, Flickr for images, and SlideShare for present-ations. Social network sites often have functionality appropriate to each of these categories; for example, although Facebook is primarily a socializing social network site, used for engaging with friends, it may also be used for navigating to content or for formal communications with colleagues. Equally, while most people use Flickr for accessing content, those in the image industry may use it for more formal communications while others may use it for more personal communications. The way social network sites are used cannot be dictated from on high, but rather emerges from the community or communities of users as they draw on the different functionalities. When a social network site tries to impose behaviour on its users, often those users are quick to move on to the next up and coming site, as occurred when the early social network site Friendster started to delete fake accounts (Boyd and Ellison, 2007).

It is important that when investigating social network sites presumptions are not made that just because two accounts are using the same social media service the people behind the accounts are trying to use the social network site in the same way. For example, a content analysis of institutional library accounts on Twitter found them to be primarily used for broadcasting news and information (Stuart, 2010). The power of social network sites is their interactive nature, the ability for librarians to engage with their patrons (Milstein, 2009; Stuart, 2010). Fields (2010) rightly pointed out that the services do not have to be restricted to interaction uses, and used a Twitter question for highlighting questions that had been asked at the reference desk; however, as the account is no longer available and was reported to have very few followers (Popegrutch, 2011) it can be seen to be difficult to sustain a non-socializing presence on a primarily socializing network.

Socializing social network sites

Socializing is the dominant purpose of the most popular social network sites in the world. Twitter and Facebook are currently estimated to have over 200 million (Twitter, 2013) and 1 billion (Facebook, 2012) active monthly users respectively. It is now quite normal to find links to institutional accounts for these services embedded on a library's home page, and visiting the main library web page for each of the 119 UK HEIs' libraries included in the *Guardian* (2012) ranking in February 2013 found 77 institutions to have Twitter accounts and 59 to have Facebook accounts prominently displayed. As can be seen in Table 5.1, two other predominantly socializing social network sites were also identified as being used: Google+ and Foursquare. Social media use, like website use more generally, can be seen to follow a power-law distribution; in the same way that a handful of websites account for a disproportionately large proportion of all web traffic, so it is not surprising to find the majority of identified social media accounts are associated with only two services.

Table 5.1 Social media accounts identified from the main library page of UK HEIs' libraries, 2013	
Social media	Number of UK HEI libraries (out of 119)
Twitter	77
Facebook	59
YouTube	21
Flickr	4
Google+	4
Foursquare	3
Vimeo	2
Pinterest	1
Google Gadget	1

The survey provides an insight into the distribution of current social media tools used by libraries within UK HEIs, and a sample of accounts for demonstrating the potential of various metrics later in the chapter. It is highly likely that many other institutional social network accounts are associated with an institution, as well as many personal accounts for the librarians working within them. At least from the perspective of public facing services, socializing social network sites are the most popular type of social network site.

This dominance may be expected. Socializing social network sites are primarily about interacting, and the establishing of profiles on such sites provides new channels for communication with a library or information service's users. The focus of web analytics for socializing social network sites is therefore likely to be focused on indications of interaction. This is reflected in following or subscribing to an account's content, and engaging with the account holder. This may include reactions to content, and should also include unsolicited content. Not all such interaction is positive, and a content analysis or sentiment analysis may be necessary to provide meaning to the metrics. Criticism can provide useful feedback for information services, although only if it is being tracked and monitored. Most organizations receive a certain amount of criticism, but it is nonetheless important that they are attuned to a spike in criticism so that it can be dealt with quickly.

Socializing social network sites encourage a wide range of discussion, and librarians should be interested not only in direct communications (comments directed at them and their content), but also the content of the social network site more generally. From a web analytics perspective this may require monitoring how people are mentioning the library and information service among one another; from a webometrics perspective it may require the monitoring of any terms that could provide insights into real-world activities. Socializing social network sites are a particularly useful source for webometric analyses as they provide the opportunity to gain insights into anything that may be the topic of conversation between two people – namely, anything. As is regularly seen in the increasing number of cases in British courts where people are prosecuted for comments they have made online, people rarely censor themselves as much as may be advisable in a public arena.

Networking social network sites

When considering appropriate metrics for networking social network sites, there is likely to be greater interest in the quality of the interactions rather than the quantity. It is not necessarily how many people who respond to a job or funding call posted on a networking social network site, but the quality of the applications and the bids that is important. It is not how many connections are made online, but how many of those transfer into real-world meetings and collaborations that is important. Often the quality of the connections is harder to quantify, although attempts may be made. Rather than focusing on the number of connections or even interactions, it may be that only multiple interactions are considered, where other users have demonstrated their perceived value of the connection by re-enforcing it many times.

It may be that the quality of the network is reflected in the diversity of connectors, building on Granovetter's (1973) notion of the strength of weak ties, where some of our most useful contacts are not our close friends with whom we might have a lot in common, but rather those connections with whom there is less shared knowledge, bringing new perspectives and ideas to any problems.

Although networking social network sites and services were not identified in the survey of UK HEIs, this may be because they are primarily personal accounts (even if they are used in a professional capacity) rather than institutional accounts. The active nature of the community of librarians on networking social network sites can often be seen, for example, on the LinkedIn group pages for organizations such as CILIP and the American Library Association.

Networking social network sites are of interest to librarians not only from an analytics perspective, but also for insights into particular communities of users. Although a networking social network site may have far less diverse content than a socializing social network site, there is also the potential for far less noise and more focused investigations on professional interactions. For example, whereas it might be possible to investigate a network of theoretical physicists on both a socializing social network site (e.g., Twitter) and a networking social network site (e.g., ResearchGate), the socializing social network site will include non-professional connections and content, and even the interactions between physicists are more likely to be of a non-professional variety. It may be the additional connections and content are of interest to the researcher, but if not, it may just be noise in the research.

Navigation social network sites

Navigation social network sites refer to those sites which support the discovery of content through social network connections. Unsurprisingly, unlike the social network sites for socializing, and social network sites for networking, the focus of social network sites for navigation is less on the number or strength of the connections (although these may be a contributory factor) and more on the creation of content and the navigation of users to it.

From a web analytics perspective librarians are interested in the impact of their content: views on YouTube, Flickr or Pinterest, and reactions to their social bookmarking websites and socially posted events. But, as with socializing and networking social network sites, they also offer the potential for wider insights: what do eBay postings and prices tell us about the economy? How do photographic choices change over time?

Atypical social media – Wikipedia

Wikipedia may be considered a social network site, at least according to Boyd and Ellison's (2007) definition, allowing users to construct a public profile in a bounded system, articulate connections to other users, and navigate the connections they, and others, make. The social network aspects are of less interest than the content that is created. Although this may also be the case with a navigation social network site, in Wikipedia the content may be considered as separate from the users who created it. While it is possible to identify the particular contributions that have been made by each user, as the page is created in an iterative fashion and is viewed as a whole, it is meaningless to consider parts of the page as distinct units with distinct authors in the same way as a YouTube video or a SlideShare presentation could be considered.

While librarians are unlikely to create an internal wiki that has sufficient data for webometric or scientometric investigations, as the sixth highest ranking website in the world (according to Alexa) Wikipedia may be considered valuable for a wide range of webometric or scientometric investigations as millions of users make contributions.

Research and tools for specific sites and services

In this section we consider some of the metrics, tools and research for some of the most popular social network sites.

Twitter

The microblogging platform and socializing social network site Twitter is one of the most popular social media services. In comparison with other social network sites the core functionality is relatively simple, focusing primarily on the publishing of 140-character status updates. The size of the 'tweet' was originally established so that the messages could be sent via the text messaging functionality of mobile phones, and openness and access to the data was incorporated into Twitter from the start to enable the building of applications for interacting with the service from different platforms. The combination of a large number of Twitter users and the 400 million daily status updates that are sent on seemingly every conceivable topic, along with a large number of accessible APIs, means that Twitter has been the focus of a large number of investigations on a wide variety of topics.

As with investigations making use of Google Trends these include many economic and public health investigation: Zhang, Fuehres and Gloor (2012) found that Twitter not only correlated with financial market movement, but could even be predictive, while Achrekar et al. (2011) found Twitter to provide a real-time indicator of flu-like illnesses. Twitter offers the potential to provide insights into a wide range of people's behaviour: Golder and Macy (2011) showed how people's mood on Twitter changes over the time of day, while the tool they created during the research process (http://timeu.se) was then used by Cunningham (2012) to show alcohol and cigarette consumption could be reflected in Twitter, and to suggest that it could be used to investigate the impact of public health policies.

The social network nature of Twitter also enables additional levels of investigation. When Himelboim, McCreery and Smith (2013) mapped Twitter networks for ten politically sensitive topics they found clusters of people of the same political persuasion. There is further discussion of Twitter as a source for relational investigations in Chapter 6.

The use of Twitter within the library community has been the focus of a number of investigations as researchers have tried to determine how libraries are using Twitter (e.g., Stuart, 2010; Del Bosque, Leif and Skarl, 2012), who is following a library's Twitter account (Sewell, 2013), and how followers are then disseminating this information to other users (Kim, Abels and Yang, 2012). Although primarily a socializing social network site, librarians have been found to use Twitter for a wide range of activities, from highlighting library resources and news to interacting with other users, and appropriate metrics for librarians investigating the impact of their own content depend heavily on their own adoption.

Twitter tools

As a result of the popularity of Twitter, and the relative openness of its data, a number of tools have been built for investigating the data. These range from tools designed to provide insights into an individual account's impact, to those designed for accessing data from the whole Twitter stream. Therefore a wide variety of investigations can be carried out without any programming skills.

At the most simple level are tools that provide an alert service, such as Tweet Beep (http://tweetbeep.com), which can alert a user to mentions of user names or websites, or Fllwrs (http://fllwrs.com), which allows a user to track who is following (and unfollowing) them over time.

Most users are not just interested in being alerted to online content, but wish to understand the impact of their account. Tweet Grader (http://tweet.grader.com) provides a simple user rank for any Twitter username that is entered, and a grade score which denotes the proportion of people graded who got a lower score according to the Tweet Grader algorithm. The algorithm is based on six factors, although Tweet Grader does not publish the weighting it accords to each of the factors: the number of followers; the power of followers (those with a high ranking in turn rank more highly); the number of updates; how recently they updated the account; follower and following recency; and engagement (e.g., retweets and mentions). There are many such services, sometimes offering some information for free and some requiring a subscription for a pro account. For example, Retweet Rank (www. retweetrank.com) provides its Retweet Rank ranking for free, but other metrics such as reach and exposure are only available to those with a pro account. The Retweet Rank ranking is based on the number of retweets, number of followers, friends and lists a user is on although, again, the weighting that is ascribed to each of those factors is not provided.

Such rankings are, to a great extent, meaningless. To discover that my Twitter account has a Retweet Rank rank of 479,011 ranking it in the 91.23 percentile or Tweet Grader rank of 1,680,937 and a grade of 88 out of 100 provides little useful information. Without understanding the weighting that is ascribed to the different rankings it is impossible to determine whether or not the rank suitably represents the purposes of the account. If a Twitter account is being used to share news it may be felt that the number of retweets is important, but if it is used primarily for addressing user queries then it may be that the number of mentions is the important metric. Rankings also require the context of similar users. With Retweet Rank and Tweet Grader this requires each of the names to be entered in turn.

More extensive and detailed investigations often require the downloading of content from Twitter for analysis. This may be achieved through the direct use of Twitter's extensive set of APIs, or desktop tools which have been built on top of these APIs. The Twitter APIs can provide access to current information about a user's network of friends, followers, tweets and other associated information, and to the whole public Twitter stream. It is possible to start gathering every tweet that meets a particular filter declaration, or a sample of public tweets. With special permission it is even possible to access the Twitter firehouse, which gives access to every tweet that is published, although this is unlikely to be appropriate in most situations. There are also tools available for downloading the information automatically. Webometric Analyst (http://lexiurl.wlv.ac.uk) allows a Twitter search to be carried out every hour and recent tweets to be downloaded, while the Excel template NodeXL (http://nodexl.codeplex.com) is designed for Twitter data networks to be downloaded. Both these tools are returned to in Chapter 6 when looking at network analysis.

Facebook

With over 1 billion active monthly users, Facebook is the world's most popular social network site. It enables the sharing of a wider range of content than the text-centric Twitter, and is also a platform for third-party tools and applications. As well as metrics based around a user's profile (e.g., the number of friends, the number of comments on a user's wall, and likes of its content), Facebook also enables the creation of pages, designed for building a community around a particular topic or institution, for which Facebook provides additional 'insights' after at least 30 people have liked a page. These insights provide additional metrics, such as the number of people who view a page, how many see a post, and the number of comments a page has received. This 'insight' data is aggregated so that individuals cannot be recognized, and if a person viewing a page is not a member of Facebook (or is not logged in) they will not be included in the analytics. In many ways pages have superseded the earlier 'groups', although groups have the advantage that they can be closed and have users join rather than merely 'like'.

Whereas Twitter had openness built in from the start, Facebook was originally private by default, and much of the information that may provide the basis of a useful web metric investigation is not available. However, for public pages some of the insight data is publicly available:

- the number of people talking about the page
- the number of people liking the page
- the most popular week
- the most popular age group
- the number of photos tagged with the page
- the most visited week
- the largest number of people visiting the page at one time.

These limited statistics nonetheless allow for comparisons to be made between multiple Facebook pages. Table 5.2 (overleaf) shows the top ten UK HEI libraries' Facebook pages as ranked by the total number of 'likes' the pages have received. Although rather than providing a definitive answer about the institution with the most successful Facebook page, it actually raises more questions: if the University of Glasgow Library has the most 'likes', why are twice as many people talking about the LSE? Why are so few photographs being associated with the University of Southampton? And what was the cause of the University of Portsmouth's exceptionally high number of visitors in a week?

Table 5.2 Facebook page statistics for the ten most liked UK HEI library pages in June 2013

Library	Total likes	People talking about this	Photos tagged here	Most visits in a week	Largest group check in
University of Glasgow	4662	45	1385	77	6
London School of Economics	4277	107	2795	130	9
Warwick University	4242	38	1339	64	10
University of Portsmouth	3282	21	2022	362	13
University of Leicester	3204	50	2360	94	14
Brunel University	2787	26	1044	87	17
Durham University	2765	25	1321	51	34
University of Southampton	2134	10	89	12	4
Staffordshire University	2012	23	Data not available		
University of Sussex	1989	41	1876	76	15

There have been thousands of academic studies focused on Facebook, although because of the nature of the diversity of the content and the differences in extracting information from the social network site these are generally concerned with the behaviour of particular sets of users or behaviour on specific pages, rather than with Facebook's potential for global indicators in the style of Google Flu Trends. For example, Zhang, He and Sang (2013) analysed 1352 messages posted in a Facebook diabetes group, while Ponce et al. (2013) investigated the public profiles of graduating medical students to determine whether they posted content that would be deemed unprofessional according to the Accreditation Council for Graduate Medical Education guidelines.

Facebook provides a rich source of content for librarians, not only for investigating the impact of their own and similar organizations' pages, but also for investigating pages of content related to their users.

Facebook tools

As with Twitter, there are services that provide a ranking of the most popular Facebook pages, based on the most number of likes or people talking about a page (e.g., www.pagedatapro.com), although as is also the case with any such rankings they should be treated with caution. Comparisons are only useful between similar types of organizations, and when pages are being used for the same purposes.

The NodeXL template (http://nodexl.codeplex.com) has additional plug-ins available (http://socialnetimporter.codeplex.com) that allow for the downloading of networks for Facebook pages, groups and personal networks. This software is returned to in the next chapter.

As is often the case, freely available public tools may not provide the necessary functionality that a researcher requires, and it can be necessary to create a bespoke tool. Facebook has a wide range of APIs (https://developers.facebook.com/docs/reference/apis/) for interacting with individual pages and the open graph. While some of the APIs require authentication, they may nonetheless be investigated with the Graph API explorer (https://developers.facebook.com/tools/explorer/).

YouTube

Librarians making use of a navigational social network site are likely to be particularly interested in how many times the content has been viewed, and this depends heavily on the functionality of the website. YouTube is a video-sharing website, and the most popular navigation social network site identified in the survey of UK HEI libraries has an extensive range of analytics available (www.youtube.com/analytics). This provides librarians interested in the impact of their own content with all the information they may wish for about views, demographics, comments, likes, dislikes, subscribers and favourites.

As well as interest from a web analytics perspective, YouTube has also been the focus of a number of academic studies. As with Facebook these studies have primarily revolved around particular topics and groups of users. Health care is a popular topic for investigation as researchers assess the accuracy of videos on various health topics, for example, inflammatory bowel disease (Mukewar et al., 2013), pediatric tonsillectomies (Strychowsky et al., 2013) and epilepsy (Wong, Stevenson and Selwa, 2013). Other areas that have been subject to recent studies include the nature of political comment on the Whitehouse YouTube channel (Halpern and Gibbs, 2013) and a library's YouTube channel as part of its wider social media offering (Vucovich et al., 2013).

There have also been more traditional informetric style investigations. Chowdhury and Makaroff (2013) investigated the growth patterns of the number of views for different categories of YouTube videos, finding that whereas early views are an indicator for future popularity for some categories they are not for others. Sugimoto et al. (2013) investigated the relationship between the presenters in TED (Technology, Entertainment, Design) talks and the impact of TED talks, measuring as views, comments and likes. Lai and Wang (2013) have investigated the impact of embedding YouTube content on external sites on the number of views a video receives.

As navigation social network sites are designed for the discovery of content it may be argued that they are of particular interest to the community of librarians, although investigations into the trustworthiness of the videos that are available for particular keywords, or the nature of the comments on particular channels, may be achieved (albeit painstakingly) without any specialized tools. Automatic data collection tools may enable more extensive investigations.

YouTube tools

As with many social network sites YouTube provides an extensive set of APIs for interrogating its content (the functionality of which may be explored through Google's API explorer (https://developers.google.com/apis-explorer), and a number of tools make use of this. Webometric Analyst (http://lexiurl.wlv.ac.uk) allows for the downloading of a wide range of content, from the information about a set of users' videos to comments associated with a set of videos, and any associated networks. The ability of Webometric Analyst to collect YouTube comments is returned to below, where it is used to form the basis of a sentiment analysis. The NodeXL template (http://nodexl.codeplex.com) also allows for the investigation of YouTube networks based on a YouTube user's network and a video's network (e.g., shared category or commentated on by shared users).

As was mentioned in Chapter 4, Google Trends also provides insights into YouTube search. Such a perspective may provide a wide range of additional investigations, and provide an additional level of analysis to the current wave of studies investigating the content of videos for particular search queries. Previously, videos may have been identified on what the researcher thought a user would search for rather than what they actually searched for.

Wikipedia

Wikipedia differs significantly from the other social media websites discussed above, with the contributions of individuals generally of less interest than the collaborative outcomes; the popularity and size of the site make it a special case, and its potential for webometric research has been recognized since 2005

(Voß, 2005). In summer 2013 it was the sixth ranked website in the world (Alexa, 2013b) and had over 4 million English language pages covering every conceivable subject.

Like YouTube, the content rather than the user is of overwhelming importance on Wikipedia, and there have been a number of articles investigating the reliability of the articles on Wikipedia in comparison with traditionally edited resources. For example, it was found to compare well for scientific articles (Giles, 2005) and articles about drugs (Clauson et al., 2008) but less well for historical articles (Rector, 2008), although Kimmons (2011) suggests that the typical article is not edited by as many editors or subject to as many revisions as would be suggested by studies that have only looked at a small selection of articles. However, the content is undeniably diverse, and also available in multiple languages, and has been used for the categorization of documents in Polish (Ciesielski et al., 2012). Wikipedia was one of two social network sites (along with the social bookmarking site Delicious) found to have a high correlation with the number of total inlinks to Spanish universities, when a range of social network sites were investigated following the discontinuation of Yahoo's 'linkdomain' functionality (Orduña-Malea and Ontalba-Ruiperez, 2013).

The breadth of Wikipedia topics means that a wide variety of topics may be investigated: a scientometric investigation may investigate how the number of Wikipedia edits or editors reflects the growth of a new field; the types of edits on a company page may reflect a positive or negative outlook for the company; or visits to health-related pages may reflect public health concerns about particular illnesses. It is important to consider the bias of editors, however, who are overwhelmingly male and based in North America or Western Europe (Wikimedia Foundation, 2011), and this may be part of the reason for the huge difference between the editing and viewing of two pages for similar events on 15 April 2013: the Boston Marathon bombings (http://en.wikipedia.org/wiki/Boston_Marathon_bombings) and a series of bombings across Iraq on the same day (http://en.wikipedia.org/wiki/15_April_2013_Iraq_attacks). Table 5.3 (overleaf) provides a comparison of the page information for the two pages five days after the attacks.

This example also shows wikimetrics may be able to provide quantifiable insights into established concepts such as newsworthiness. Obviously there are more differences between the two sets of bombings besides the number of dead and injured and their geographic location, most noticeably because the Iraq attacks were part of an ongoing insurgency whereas the Boston bombings were unexpected, and the Boston bombings were an ongoing news story as the hunting

Table 5.3 Wikimetrics for two bombings on 15 April 2013		
	.../15_April_2013_Iraq_attacks	.../Boston_Marathon_bombings
Dead	≥75 3	3
Injured	>350	183
Number of edits	106	3808
Number of distinct authors	36	663
Number of page views	12,909	422,520

down of the bombers was played out across the news. Nevertheless it is easy to see how a more extensive study could take into consideration a far wider variety of variables to investigate newsworthiness of different topics over time.

Wikipedia tools

Importantly the history of every edit of every page of Wikipedia is publicly visible and page views have also been made publicly available (http://dumps.wikimedia.org/other/pagecounts-raw).This has enabled a number of tools to be created to gain insights into Wikipedia usage:

- *Wikitrends* (http://toolserver.org/~johang/wikitrends) – shows the most popular pages on Wikipedia, as well as those most rapidly rising and falling in popularity, for the current day, week or month for each language version of Wikipedia
- *Wikipedia Article Traffic Statistics* (http://stats.grok.se) – provides access to traffic statistics for any particular page
- *Wikipedia Page History Statistics* (http://vs.aka-online.de/cgi-bin/wppagehiststat.pl) – summarizes information about the edits that a Wikipedia page has received, showing when edits took place and who made most of the edits
- *Editor Interaction Analyzer* (http://toolserver.org/~snottywong/editorinteract.html) – allows multiple editors to be compared to find other pages they have worked on.

There is also a NodeXL (http://nodexl.codeplex.com) plug-in that enables MediaWiki networks to be explored (http://wikiimporter.codeplex.com). This enables the simple creation of networks based on hyperlinks between articles and author contributions.

Figure 5.3 shows the Wikipedia article network based on outlinks from the webometrics page. Although Wikipedia makes a lot of data available, that information is not necessarily available in a format that is most useful to someone wanting to carry out the analysis. Instead it may be necessary to visit a page and collect the data manually, or revisit the same page on a number of different occasions.

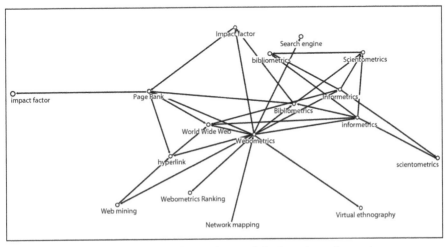

Figure 5.3 Wikipedia article network based on outlinks from the webometrics page

Other social network sites

Discussions about social media often note the huge variety of sites, and then proceed to focus solely on either Twitter or Facebook. As was seen in the survey of UK HEI libraries, there is a clear long tail when it comes to social media usage, although there is little point in discussing each of the sites in detail. Nevertheless these other social network sites have formed the basis of many academic studies, including some that have focused in particular on the library community.

Thornton (2012) has investigated the use of Pinterest in academic libraries. Kwan and Chan (2009) investigated the potential of linking the folksonomy of the social bookmarking site Delicious with Library of Congress Subject Headings. Angus, Thelwall and Stuart (2008) investigated the usefulness of tags in Flickr to determine its potential as an academic image resource. Even if the social network site's content is not of interest to the researcher, the network may be used to solicit opinions. For example, Oyelude and Bamigbola (2012) used LinkedIn to survey people on their opinions on the role of the library. Any of these may be the focus of an investigation by a librarian, either for web analytic purposes or webometric purposes.

URL shorteners – web analytic links on any site

Metrics on third-party services may change with little or no notice, suddenly reducing the insights that librarians can have into the impact that their content is making. One way around this in certain situations is to make use of a URL shortening service. Depending on a website's design and the particular content management system a particular URL may be extremely long, running to hundreds of characters in length. These extremely long URLs can be difficult for people to share, either because the communication medium reformats the content (e.g., an e-mail platform may split a URL over multiple lines) or the platform limits the space available for communication (e.g., Twitter restricts user messages to 140 characters), and URL shortening services were developed to ease the process of sharing URLs. A URL shortening service provides a short URL, which when visited redirects users to the original URL.

The redirecting process not only allows the sharing of awkwardly long URLs, but also provides content providers with the opportunity to gather information about users as they travel from one site to another. For example, a librarian may wish to share a link to an interesting article a third party has posted online. Without access to the server logs or web analytics of the target website they are restricted to any metrics that Facebook may make available about the number of people clicking on a link. If a URL shortening service is utilized, however, information way be gathered about users as they click through.

Bit.ly, the most popular URL shortening service, provides access to how often a particular shortened URL has been visited, how other people have shared a shortened URL, the number of times a URL has been clicked on, where the referring URL is, and the location of users (see Figure 5.4).

URL shortening services are not an unmitigated good, however, and librarians should consider the ramifications of using URL shortening services, as they should for their use of any online content they create, for example, the potential problems of link decay if a URL shortening service is discontinued or changes its policies.

Top Countries (clicks / % of total)		
United States	35	34%
United Kingdom	25	25%
Argentina	4	4%
Canada	3	3%
Spain	2	2%
Sweden	2	2%
Netherlands	2	2%
Singapore	1	1.0%
Belgium	1	1.0%
No location detected	24	24%
+3 more		

Figure 5.4 Geographic distribution of clicks for a BBC News story as seen through Bit.ly

General social media impact

As well as sites offering a ranking or a grade for an account on a specific social network service such as Twitter, there are additional sites that offer to analyse the impact of an individual's or organization's profile across multiple sites. For example, Klout (http://klout.com) provides a single score from 1 to 100 based on data from a wide range of social network sites. These include not only socializing social network sites such as Facebook and Twitter, but also networking social network sites (e.g., LinkedIn), navigation social network sites (e.g., YouTube, Flickr and LastFM) and blogging sites (e.g., Tumblr, Blogger and Wordpress). As with the simplistic rankings of a single site, a global social media ranking does not necessarily reflect the use to which the social media is being put in a specific institution and encourages comparison with different types of organization. In addition, an overall social media ranking may encourage certain behaviour on a particular platform to increase their ranking, and the use of services that are inappropriate. For example, for most librarians a LastFM network is unlikely to be an integral part of delivering user services, although if a Klout score is used to judge the impact of their social media offering they may be tempted to spend time on it.

Another general social media grading site that is worthy of note is Wefollow (http://wefollow.com). Like Klout it provides a ranking on a scale of 1 to 100; this 'prominence' rank is based on a PageRank style networking of Twitter, Facebook, Instagram and LinkedIn. Unlike Klout it allows users to express their interests, so librarians could compare themselves with others who have stated they are librarians or have an interest in libraries. Nevertheless, any such rankings should only ever be taken as a bit of fun and never given any credence.

Sentiment analysis

One of the big advantages of social network sites is that they provide access to a large quantity of data that is structured in a similar fashion. This means that sentiment analysis may be applied across large quantities of data, determining with human levels of accuracy whether texts are positive or negative. In many instances content analysis is still the most appropriate method, either because the question that needs to be answered is not about sentiment, or the media type is not suitable for sentiment analysis (e.g., video and images). It may also be the case that for many of the instances where a librarian wishes to determine sentiment (e.g., comments on the content they have posted themselves), it may be a small enough sample for them to carry out an analysis by hand. Nevertheless, there are instances when a larger scale sentiment analysis is necessary.

As Twitter is increasingly recognized as a potential source of indicators on a wide range of topics, from the state of the economy to public health, it is not surprising to find that there are a number of services that provide sentiment analysis of recent tweets for particular search terms. For example, Sentiment140 (www.sentiment140.com) provides quick access to the sentiment associated with recent tweets for a particular term or phrase. Another Twitter sentiment analysis service (http://smm.streamcrab.com) not only provides analysis of recent tweets, but also monitors tweets as they are published, more suitable for popular or trending topics. Although Twitter may be considered the pulse of the web, there are many other social media services that are of interest to sentiment analysis. Social Mention (http://socialmention.com) provides insights into the sentiment of a host of different content (e.g., social bookmarks, news stories, comments and images) and even allows the data to be downloaded.

As with so much of the work, while there is a certain amount that may be achieved through web-based tools, greater analysis often requires the processing power of software on the computer desktop. There is an active community of developers working around sentiment analysis, but while there is a lot of computer code and lexical resources available, there are few freely available tools that are accessible to non-technical computer users. One that is freely available for non-commercial use is SentiStrength (http://sentistrength.wlv.ac.uk), from the Statistical Cybermetrics Group at the University of Wolverhampton. Using files of weighted terms, which may be calibrated either automatically or by hand to reflect the idiosyncrasies of a particular data set, SentiStrength can automatically classify the sentiments of a set of texts in a plain text file with one text per line.

There are a number of different approaches to sentiment analysis; for example Sentiment140 takes a machine learning approach based on an analysis of tweets that include emoticons (Go, Bhayani and Huang, 2009), whereas others make use of lexicons where words have been ascribed a particular sentiment (e.g., SentiWordNet; http://sentiwordnet.isti.cnr.it). As is frequently pointed out, some texts are more suitable for sentiment analysis than others, and some texts may be more appropriate to certain approaches to sentiment analysis than others. It is therefore important to investigate the accuracy of a sentiment analysis tool with a particular data set before it forms the basis of a large-scale investigation or any significant decisions are made based on the analysis by a particular tool.

Nevertheless, appropriate sentiment analysis software enables a wide range of investigations to be made. For example, in the case study below Webometric Analyst and SentiStrength are used to carry out a quick investigation to explore whether people are reacting positively to academic libraries' online videos. Sentiment analysis is not suitable for every situation, but it is undoubtedly a useful tool for the automatic analysis of the vast quantities of data that are increasingly available to researchers, although for robust results it is important that the software is tested and calibrated for a particular data set.

A YOUTUBE CASE STUDY

In the survey of UK HEI library websites, 21 were identified as having links to a YouTube presence. Of these, seven were library videos hosted as part of a wider institutional account, and data was collected from the remaining 14 accounts.

Through the creation of a simple text document listing the user names of the 14 accounts, Webometric Analyst can quickly gather data from all the data associated with those accounts. This merely requires the 'Search by User Name' option and clicking on the 'Searching For Videos Matching Each Query in File' button, before directing the pop-up window to direct the program to the relevant file of user names. An additional file is then created containing information about the most recent 1000 videos associated with each of those accounts, and the associated statistics for each (e.g., likes, dislikes, duration of the video and number of comments). The 14 accounts had 430 videos between them. YouTube allows three levels of user control over comments: allowed (the default), moderated and denied. Nine of the videos did not allow comments and 24 were moderated (requiring approval before they were published). Of the 421 that could have had comments, only 21 actually did and the majority of them only had one comment: one video had six comments, two videos had five comments, two videos had four comments, one video had three comments, two videos had two comments and 13 had one comment.

The published comments were downloaded by creating a text file of video IDs from the results of the previous query, and then selecting 'YouTube comments for List of Video IDs' in Webometric Analyst. This resulted in 36 comments, two that were not in English, and one spam, which could then be analysed in SentiStrength by selecting 'Sentiment Strength Analysis' and then 'Analyse ALL texts in file'. The regular version provides two sentiment scores for each text, both a positive sentiment (1 to 5) and negative sentiment (−1 to −5). The Java version also allows for single scale (−4 to +4), binary (positive or negative) and trinary (positive, negative or neutral) analysis. Figure 5.5 shows the sentiments of the library videos, with the size of the bubble representing the number of videos that adhered to the position. As can be seen, most of the comments were not negative (−1) but may be considered fairly positive (2 or 3). ∎

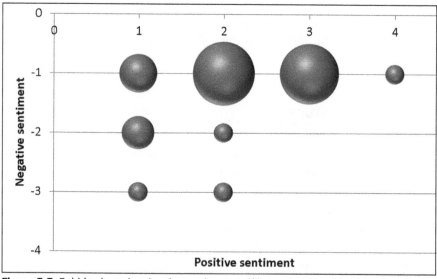

Figure 5.5 Bubble chart showing the sentiments of library videos on YouTube

Conclusion

Social media technologies are used in many different ways, and it is important not to dismiss a technology just because it did not work in one particular instance. Although there is a lot of discussion about the range of social media sites and services that are available, a handful of websites and services account for the vast majority of social media usage. While this may be considered a negative, with monopolies reducing user-choice and allowing the largest social media companies to act with a degree of impunity, it is also important to recognize the advantages it provides to web metric research as social media sites provide vast amounts of structured data. A service like Twitter, which has hundreds of millions of users updating their status multiple times a day, now allows for insights into the mood and opinions of people in real time, the 'pulse' of the connected world, to adopt the title of Hubbard's (2011) book.

From a webometric perspective social network sites are an unquestionable good: vast quantities of structured data are now available for analysis as people increasingly upload information about more and more aspects of their lives. That does not mean that the same services are a useful part of the librarians' online activities and web analytics are important for determining whether the tools are contributing to a librarian's work. Potential and reality are not always the same thing, especially when it comes to emerging technologies; while in theory social networks sites should be useful tools for students, a survey found time spent on social network sites to be a negative indicator of academic performance (Paul, Baker and Cochran, 2012).

6

Investigating relationships between actors

Introduction

Relational web metrics investigate the relationships between online actors, whether these are individuals, organizations, Twitter accounts or web pages. They may be considered distinct from evaluative web metrics as they are not necessarily designed to provide insights into the impact of content, but rather provide insights into the structure of the network as a whole, or the position of actors within a network. As has been pointed out already, the distinction between evaluative and relational metrics may merely be one of perception; being central to a network may be considered an indicator of impact, or may merely be an indicator of being central to the network.

This chapter considers some of the social network analysis methodologies that have been adopted by the web metrics community and how these methodologies and visualization technologies may be used to draw insights that may be of use for librarians.

Social network analysis methods

Social network analysis methodologies were developed in the social sciences based on the idea that actors should not be considered in isolation, but rather that their behaviour was best understood within the context of connected actors. The importance of people's social networks for sharing information and changing user behaviours is now widely recognized (Christakis and Fowler, 2009), and the application of social network analysis methodologies have not only been suggested for the information science community for traditional bibliometric investigations (Otte and Rousseau, 2002), but also formed the basis of webometric investigations analysing the hyperlinks between web pages (e.g., Park, Barnett and Nam, 2002; Holmberg, 2009).

Although social network analysis methodologies may be applied to the web and information on it, it has a far broader set of applications, so the terminology generally used is one of nodes and edges rather than web pages and hyperlinks. A network (or graph) comprises nodes (sometimes referred to as vertices) and edges, which are the connections between nodes. These edges may be undirected or directed (in which case they may be referred to as arcs) depending on the nature of the connection. For example, web pages are connected by directional links, and just because a blog links to a BBC news story does not mean that the BBC story automatically links back to the blog. In comparison, friendship edges (at least in the physical world) are generally considered to be undirected: if person A is friends with person B then person B is also friends with person A.

As well as graphs being either directed or undirected, they may also be binary or weighted. For example, on Twitter, following is a binary relationship – an account either follows another account or it does not – whereas there may be any number of messages sent between two Twitter accounts and an analysis of a graph may weight relationships according to the number of messages sent between two users.

Network analysis measures may be characterized as one of three types: measures for the property of nodes and edges, those that describe the neighbourhood of a node, and those that analyse the structure of the entire network (Börner, Sanyal and Vespignani, 2007). This chapter is not designed to be an exhaustive introduction to the topic of social network analysis, but rather demonstrate the potential of network analysis techniques to librarians. This section focuses on three areas: node centrality, cluster analysis and statistical properties of the graph. Each may provide valuable insights to librarians and may be visualized and analysed through many different social network analysis software packages that are available. Some come at a price (e.g. UCINet), some are available for free (e.g., Pajek) and some are open source (e.g., Gephi). Within this chapter two pieces of software are used: NodeXL, because of its ease of use for downloading content from the web and visualizing networks; and Gephi, because its extensive range of plug-ins makes it suitable in a wide range of situations.

Node centrality

Rather than investigating the centrality of a node within the structure of the whole of a graph, most early webometric investigations evaluated the impact of a web document based on the inlinks from the immediate vicinity.

However, a far wider variety of analytical methods has been developed within social network analysis, and been expanded by information scientists and computer scientists; they have since been applied to networks of web documents and social media accounts.

There have been a wide variety of centrality measurements devised, the most established and traditionally the most important of which have been degree centrality, closeness centrality and betweenness centrality. More recently there has been growing interest in eigenvector centrality, in particular PageRank, which may be considered a variation of it. Each of the different measures of centrality attempt to measure different aspects of the relationship between the node and the network:

- The *degree* centrality of a node is based on the number of direct connections it has with other nodes; this is the equivalent of the crude counting of inlinks and outlinks in early webometric studies.
- *Closeness centrality* recognizes a node as central to a network if it can quickly interact with all other nodes.
- *Betweenness centrality* recognizes a node as central if it lies on the shortest route between other pairs of nodes.
- *Eigenvector centrality* and *PageRank* give a high centrality to those nodes that are connected to other highly connected nodes.

There is no measure of centrality that should be considered better than another, although some centrality measures may be more suitable for particular situations. Google's PageRank may be a more useful algorithm for ranking web pages than degree centrality because of the high variability in the quality of web pages and the publicly available nature of the network. However, where there is less disparity in the value of nodes, and greater difficulty in acquiring additional information about the whole network, it may be that degree centrality is a more useful measure of centrality. Equally, whereas degree centrality, PageRank and eigenvector centrality may be deemed to provide insight into variations of the 'recognition' granted to a node, recognition is not always the most important aspect. Closeness centrality may be considered particularly important in situations where people are interested in receiving or sharing information as fast as possible, whereas betweenness centrality may be a better indicator of the importance of a node to a network.

Cluster identification

The online world is no more homogenous than society at large: websites with shared interests may link to one another; social network site users with shared interests may follow one another; and people who know one another in the real world may friend one another in a virtual world. These preferences produce clusters or communities and identification of these clusters has many practical uses, both as a subject of analysis and for the dissemination of information.

Clustering in social network analysis breaks down a network into smaller networks, or clusters, based on the link structure of the network, with clusters generally being characterized as having more edges within a cluster than outside. Network analysis software may have clustering algorithms included; for instance the open source software Gephi includes both the Markov Cluster Algorithm and the Louvain Modularity method.

Applying a clustering algorithm to a network allows the identification of clusters that may not be known, or even greater insights where clustering is already known. For example, Figure 6.1 shows the network of the 79 UK MPs who were on Twitter in 2009. It is laid out according to the Force Atlas 2 algorithm included in Gephi, in which nodes repulse one another and edges try to pull nodes together. Each of the three main UK political parties is shown with a different shade (with the white nodes reflecting those affiliated with other parties), and the nodes of the political parties can be seen to cluster together.

Applying the Louvain modularity method to the network, which identifies clusters that have many edges within clusters rather than between them, also broadly clusters the MPs according to political party (see Figure 6.2). However, while the Liberal Democrats and Conservatives are identified as distinct groups, the Labour MPs actually form two groups. For those interested in Labour Party unity it is a clustering that may initiate further investigation: does the clustering reflect ideological differences? Is it reflective of a geographical difference? Or is it merely an anomaly caused by the larger number of Labour MPs using Twitter at the time?

Similar studies may provide new insights into the differences between official organizational structures and communications between employees or the differences between scientific disciplines expressed in journals and those shown in the network of scientists.

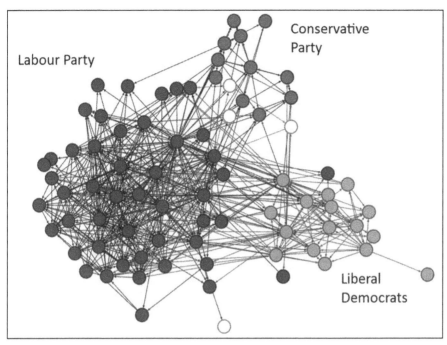

Figure 6.1 UK MPs shaded according to party affiliation

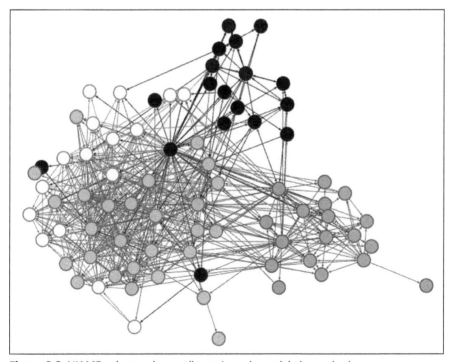

Figure 6.2 UK MPs clustered according to Louvain modularity method

Statistical properties of the graph

As well as nodes' positions within a graph, the graphs themselves may also be analysed: structural differences between networks may be considered for different sets of actors making use of the same technologies, or the same actors making use of different technologies. There are many metrics for providing insights into the overall structure of a graph, but while they may measure similar features subtle differences are likely to mean that one metric is more suitable than another.

Average centrality

As was discussed above, there are various different measures of centrality (e.g., degree centrality, betweenness centrality and closeness centrality) and average centrality may be used to provide an indicator of whether the nodes in one network are more connected than the nodes in another, or whether the nodes in one network can more quickly interact on average with the other nodes in the network than those in another network can.

Graph density

A graph's density is calculated by dividing the actual number of edges within a graph by the maximum number of possible edges in a graph. For example, in a directed graph with ten nodes the maximum number of edges is 90 as every node may link to every other node, so if the graph includes 45 edges then the graph's density is 0.5. Although graph density is related to degree centrality, one may be more suitable than the other depending on the size of the graph. For example, on a very large graph (e.g., the world wide web) graph density is inevitably very low and it is more meaningful to discuss the average degree centrality, whereas with very small networks greater insights may be achieved through providing information about the density of the network.

Clustering coefficient

The clustering of nodes within real-world graphs has often been found to create the small world phenomena where large networks of nodes nonetheless only have a few steps between any two nodes on average. The network clustering coefficient generally comes in two varieties (Hardiman and Katzir, 2013): the average clustering coefficient and the global clustering coefficient. For each node a local clustering coefficient may be calculated, reflecting the proportion of a node's neighbours that could be connected that are connected, and the average clustering coefficient is the average for all the nodes in a network. The global clustering coefficient compares the number of open triplets in a graph (where three nodes are joined by two edges) with the number of closed triplets in a graph (where three nodes are joined by three edges).

Modularity

Modularity measures the strength of clusters in a network, with a network with a high modularity having many edges within clusters rather than between them. Certain clustering algorithms, such as the Louvain modularity method used in the Twitter example above, use modularity to optimize the clustering process.

Sources for relational network analysis

The web is filled with networks that may form, and indeed have formed, the basis of a relational network analysis, including relations that are deliberately and explicitly stated, and those that emerge from the data. Within traditional bibliometrics a limited number of direct relationships were expressed, formed by co-authorship and citation networks, with many additional investigations being based around indirect relationships, for example, bibliographic coupling (two papers being linked if they cite one or more other articles) and co-citation analysis (two papers being linked if they are cited by one or more other articles). Early webometric investigations applied similar citation analysis methodologies to web pages and the hyperlinks between them: co-linked analysis is analogous with co-citation analysis (Larson, 1996) and co-link analysis is analogous to bibliographic coupling (Thelwall and Wilkinson, 2004). The data that is available online is far richer than that which was traditionally available in bibliographic databases, while social network sites have emerged that enable the investigation of a far wider range of direct relationships as well as an increasing variety of indirect relationships.

Relational web metric investigations have used links between the web pages of different types of organization to investigate relationships between the organizations (Stuart and Thelwall, 2006; Minguillo and Thelwall, 2012). A co-link analysis of Canadian university websites was used to investigate linguistic and cultural differences between French-speaking and English-speaking Canada (Vaughan, 2006), while Bar-Ilan and Azoulay (2013) investigated the structure and linking between non-profit websites in Israel. Relational analysis of social network sites has often focused on Twitter as the network has been the most open, with politics being a particularly popular area for investigation. For example, Hsu and Park (2012b) compared the networks of Korean politicians on Twitter, as well as through their blogs and their home pages, and Bruns and Highfield (2013) investigated political networks on Twitter during the Queensland state elections. Importantly, relational web metrics not only enable the investigation of existing relationships, but may also be used to identify new relationships; for example Kazienko et al. (2013) suggest social network sites for identifying new business clients.

Some of the tools and methodologies discussed are now explored with data from two sources: the web and the social network site Twitter.

WEB NETWORK ANALYSIS – LOCAL GOVERNMENT IN THE MIDLANDS

Social network sites have been gaining far more attention than traditional web pages in recent years as hundreds of millions of users have flocked to join them. There is, however, a fundamentally different kind of relationship expressed on web pages than on social network sites, and a far more diverse set of content.

As was discussed in Chapter 3, the collection of information about the linking practices between websites has become more difficult as search engines have depreciated certain link functionality and reduced access to their APIs. It nonetheless continues to be possible to investigate URL citations through the Bing API, and this is used in this example as data is gathered for visualizing the interlinking between local government organizations in the midlands in the UK. A librarian may wish to carry out such an investigation for the purposes of gaining insights into the players within a particular field, or even subsidiaries of a similar company.

URL citation-based relational investigations require the sending of a large number of queries to a search engine. It is feasible for an impact study to enter the search queries into a search engine manually, for example an impact assessment of 100 different websites could be based on 100 search engine queries. However, if URL citation or web mentions are used for some sort of network analysis, anything but the smallest of studies is likely to necessitate the automatic collection of data from a search engine. To investigate the URL citations between 100 different URLs would require entering 9900 queries, as for each of the 100 URLs a query would have to be created to determine whether it was cited within each of the other 99 websites.

The Bing API currently allows for only 5000 queries a month for free, although there is more extensive access for those with a subscription. Although librarians may wish to write their own program to make use of this data, by far the easiest way to collect data is through Webometric Analyst (http://lexiurl.wlv.ac.uk), a tool for webometric analysis from the Statistical Cybermetrics Research Group at the University of Wolverhampton, designed for collecting data from a wide variety of resources including Bing. As it is designed specifically for the webometrics community it can not only send queries to Bing automatically, but it can also create the necessary queries automatically for many of the most popular studies.

Figure 6.3 shows a URL citation network diagram for interlinking between local government institutions in two regions of the UK, the East Midlands and the West Midlands, as seen through the Bing API. To create such a network diagram it is necessary first to have a list of URLs that need to be investigated. The selection of such pages is often glossed over in webometric investigations, although it needs to be approached methodologically if a meaningful study is to be carried out. In this case, the interlinking of local government institutions includes a known set of organizations, each with a distinct URL. For other, similar studies, such as an investigation into the interlinking of local businesses in an area, there is unlikely to be an authoritative list, and decisions need to be made about how such a list is created. In this case Openly Local (http://openlylocal.com), a website for making

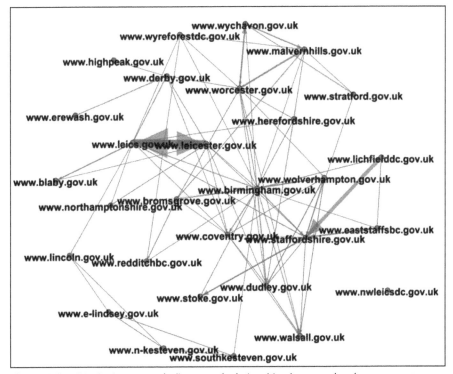

Figure 6.3 URL citation network diagram of relationships between local government organizations in the UK Midlands

local government data more accessible, was used to provide an authoritative list of institutions and a source of URLs. As the local government information is available in an XML format, the URLs could be automatically extracted using Google Docs `=importXML()` function. Once the list of URLs is saved in a text document, and a developer key has been requested for the Bing Search API, the queries can be created and the data automatically collected with Webometric Analyst in a few minutes. Although Webometric Analyst allows for the rudimentary display of network diagrams, the format in which it stores the results is also compatible with other graph visualization software such as Gephi (https://gephi.org) and Pajek (http://pajek.imfm.si/doku.php), which have greater functionality. In this instance the graph has been displayed with Gephi.

Once the data is available in Gephi a wide range of statistics may be quickly generated regarding centrality, clustering and modularity. It is important for librarians to recognize that just because a metric can be calculated, it does not mean that a metric should be calculated. It may be that all is necessary is a visualization as an aid to further investigation of the relationships between the represented parties. ■

TWITTER NETWORK ANALYSIS – UK HEI LIBRARIES ON TWITTER

The previous example required the use of multiple tools: from creating a list of websites to investigate, through gathering the data, to visualizing the results. Social network sites have increased not only the amount of structured data available on the web, but also the number of people interested in their own social graph. This has resulted in tools such as NodeXL (http://nodexl.codeplex.com), which provide a single tool for the end-to-end investigation of some of the most popular social network sites.

This example considers the network formed by the 77 Twitter accounts identified in the survey of UK HEI libraries. In this case the network is based on a survey of library websites, but NodeXL also provides the functionality for importing Twitter users' networks based on a user's network of friends, people mentioning a particular term, as well as those on a Twitter list. As Twitter users with a wide range of expertise have compiled Twitter lists on every conceivable topic, there is a wide selection of samples ready for analysis. A few that may be of interest for those wishing to experiment with NodeXL and look at how accounts link and cluster, include:

- 1270 UK Librarians (https://twitter.com/philbradley/uk-librarians)
- 458 UK Members of Parliament (https://twitter.com/tweetminster/ukmps)
- 415 UK Team GB Olympic Athletes (https://twitter.com/ACMLDN2012/team-gb-olympics-athletes).

Figure 6.4 shows the interlinking of the 77 UK HEI Library accounts using NodeXL.

The five accounts with the most followers on Twitter overall are the Bodleian Library, the library of the University of South Wales, Cambridge University Library, the University of Manchester Library and University of Sussex Library. However, when looking solely at the network of UK HEI libraries, a different set of dominant websites emerge (see Table 6.1).

The Bodleian Library and the library of the University of South Wales are not ranked in the top five for either degree centrality or betweenness centrality within the network of 77 HEI libraries, and only the University of Sussex Library is ranked in the top five for degree centrality and betweenness centrality. Although the University of Lincoln Library is followed by only ten of the other libraries in the network, it has an exceptionally high betweenness centrality because of the large number of other libraries it follows, following 45 out of a possible 76.

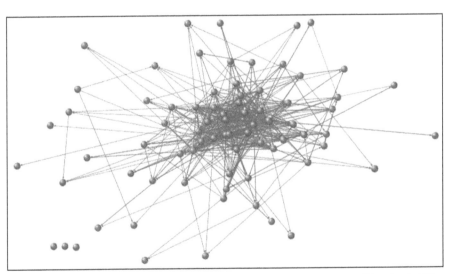

Figure 6.4 Network diagram of relationships between Twitter accounts of libraries in UK HEIs using NodeXL

Table 6.1 UK HEI's libraries with the highest degree and betweenness centrality

Rank	Degree centrality		Betweenness centrality	
1	Leeds Metropolitan	29	University of Lincoln	1337
2	University of Manchester	27	City University	545
3	Cambridge University	23	Leeds Metropolitan	453
4	City University	23	University of Sussex	401
5	University of Sussex Durham University	22 22	University of Liverpool	240

Calculating the degree centrality and betweenness centrality of the nodes provides different insights into the relationships of UK HEI libraries on Twitter. It may be argued that the degree centrality between similar organizations is a better indicator of quality of the Twitter stream than total followers, as it has less to do with reputation and student numbers, while the betweenness centrality provides a better indicator of an account engaging with the community. The average degree centrality for the graph shown in Figure 6.4 is 8.31, which may be considered relatively high for such a large geographically dispersed set of organizations. In comparison, the similar sized set of MPs had an average degree of 9.95, which while larger is not that much larger considering most of the MPs were members of the same party and can regularly be found within the same building. ■

Conclusion

This chapter introduces a number of different tools and methodologies for investigating relational web metrics, although in many ways it barely scratches the surface of relational web metrics, focusing as it has on the social network analysis approach and direct links between actors rather than some of the less direct connections that have been the focus of the bibliometric tradition in the form of bibliographic coupling and co-citation, and co-citation analysis and co-linked analysis. Nevertheless it should have given librarians some ideas about where relational web metrics may be used in their professional activities, and some of the tools and data sources that are available.

As has been emphasized elsewhere, many of the metrics discussed in this chapter may be applied for evaluative purposes: someone may wish to use betweenness centrality as an indicator of engagement within a social network, or the densities of different networks as indicators of the value of the networks. Although as was seen with the UK HEIs' libraries' Twitter accounts, different metrics inevitably emphasize different aspects of a network, and one is not necessarily better than another. In an age increasingly dominated by evaluative metrics, there is much to learn from the descriptive nature of relational metrics.

7

Exploring traditional publications in a new environment

Introduction

As we explained in Chapter 2, the term 'web bibliometrics' is used within this book to refer to the intersection between bibliometrics and web metrics, and involves the quantitative investigation of traditional publications (e.g., journals and books) through the web.

Traditional bibliometric investigations have not interrogated a universal library containing all bibliographic material that has ever been written, but rather are operationalized through a limited bibliographic resource, most often the Web of Science citation index. Such a bibliographic resource is restricted to a small proportion of the items that would be included within a universal library, and the information stored about the items is also restricted.

The web has made traditional bibliographic resources more accessible and extended potential bibliometric investigations in three ways. It:

- potentially provides access to a greater proportion of items than would be housed in a universal library
- can provide access to the full text rather than just metadata
- enables the analysis of bibliographic content within the context of how it is being used.

These extensions to traditional bibliometrics can potentially facilitate the provision of better services by librarians, through the provision of more detailed maps of science or the development of altmetrics measuring the impact of traditional publications online.

This chapter investigates each of these three areas of web bibliometrics and looks more closely at some of the research that has taken place and resources available.

More bibliographic items

Within this work use of the term 'bibliometrics' is restricted to the spirit of its Greek stem, 'biblio', and relates to the quantitative analysis of books, journals and similar types of publication that would traditionally have formed the basis of a paper-based publication. By keeping its more restrictive meaning it may seem as though by definition there are no new objects for investigation, but the vast majority of publications were never included within the bibliographic databases that formed the basis of many previous investigations.

The creation of bibliographic databases such as the Science Citation Index has traditionally been very resource intensive and it was therefore in the interests of abstracting and indexing services to limit the number of publications that were included. Bradford's law states that articles pertinent to a particular field will be widely distributed among a large number of journals, with exponentially diminishing returns as you move further away from the core journals (De Bellis, 2009), while Garfield's law of concentration further argues that the overlap between disciplines means that the core literature for the whole of science is scattered in no more than 1000 journals (Garfield, 1983). It can therefore be argued that the core scientific literature can be covered by the necessarily limited number of journals within a bibliographic database.

There are serious limitations with such an approach, however. Journal articles are by no means the only publication type, nor even the main publication type in many fields. For example, in the arts and the humanities monographs have been considered the most important type of publication, while in computer science conference proceedings have a significant role. Even if journal publications are the primary means of publication, articles will not necessarily be published among the 'core' scientific journals; new and emerging fields may instead appear in fringe and less well known publications.

This is also a very scholarly vision of publishing. For organizations from other sections of society, such as those in industry or the public sector, grey literature can have a greater role. Grey literature refers to less formally published documents, including a wide range of reports from government departments, think tanks and other organizations.

As the web has become an increasingly important publishing platform for organizations of every type, some publications that would once have been difficult to track down may now be easily found through the new generation of specialized bibliographic search engines.

Google Scholar

Probably the most famous and widely used of the new bibliographic tools, and one of the best examples of the new bibliographic ecosystem, is Google Scholar (http://scholar.google.com), which repurposes the minimal search box that originally distinguished its search engine to provide a simple way to search a wide range of scholarly literature from across the web. It offers access to a wide range of journal articles, books, abstracts, theses and grey literature. Multiple different versions of the same paper can be found alongside one another. High quality peer-reviewed journal articles may be found next to the outputs from think tanks or theses from MA students.

Since its launch Google Scholar has become an increasingly complex environment. It not only allows for the searching of scholarly documents, and provides citation information about those documents, but also provides functionality more typical of a social network site. Users are now invited to create profiles, expressing their research interests and affiliated institutions, and listing their publications. The listing of publications enables the automatic calculation of the number of citations as well as two other author metrics, the *h*-index and *i10*-index. Google Scholar also invites users to express relationships with other researchers in the form of public co-authors, as well as allowing the private following of other authors' new articles or citations, providing researchers with a new indicator of impact: the number of followers they receive on Google Scholar. This would seem quite a limited metric for the moment, as most researchers either have no profile or no followers.

Google Scholar also provides two additional ways for users to discover content. 'My updates' provides recommendations based on a user's citations, and 'metrics' enables users to browse the top publications according to language and category, with the most cited publications within each journal also listed in rank order.

Google Scholar brings bibliometrics to researchers and information professionals searching for scholarly works like never before. Authors, journals and articles are all seen in the context of their citation metrics. The ranking and recommendation algorithms are hidden to users, but nonetheless influence the works that users see, perpetuating the so-called Matthew effect, whereby the rich get richer and the poor get poorer.

Undoubtedly, as a search tool Google Scholar provides access to documents that would otherwise have been difficult to identify, and is regularly found to compare positively with the traditional citation databases for general literature searches (e.g., Beckmann and von Wehrden, 2012) and cited reference searches (e.g., Bergman, 2012). However, the automated approach to the inclusion of data not only increases the quantity of data, but also introduces data of dubious value for bibliometric purposes. Aguillo (2012) points out that the over-representation of popular scientific literature and teaching materials in Google Scholar means that bibliometric results are not comparable with traditional bibliometric databases, and although recent developments to Google Scholar make it more useful for citation analysis, it is still not recommended for promotion and hiring decisions (Jacso, 2012). Nevertheless, Google Scholar is used for bibliometric investigations (Wagstaff and Culyer, 2012).

That Google Scholar bibliometric results are not comparable to traditional bibliometrics services does not negate its value, however. Rather it should be seen as providing additional, complementary metrics that provide new insights into research impact, whether the impact among the more diverse publication types identified by Aguillo (2012), or the impact of formats that have traditionally been under-represented by traditional bibliometric databases. Kousha, Thelwall and Rezaie (2011) found that online book citations were more numerous than those found in traditional databases, and suggested that they could be used to support research evaluation.

Google Scholar is a potential source for evaluative and relational web bibliometrics. Ortega and Aguillo (2013) concluded that it was suitable for collaboration studies, and for creating a map of science based on keywords (Ortega and Aguillo, 2012). Extracting the data from Google Scholar is not simple, as currently there is not an API available. Nonetheless, the potential value of the data means that people have created tools for extracting the data.

The software program Publish or Perish (www.harzing.com/pop.htm) has been developed for the downloading of citation data from Google Scholar, facilitating access to results from Google Scholar searches, and providing access to citation metrics. Importantly, Publish or Perish restricts results to first-level queries only. For example, while it is possible to retrieve the number of citations that a set of documents has received, it does not allow for the automatic retrieval of the citing documents, so that the acceptable use of Google Scholar is not exceeded, and users do not find themselves temporarily barred from the service. Unfortunately this makes it difficult to carry out more extensive analysis, for example taking into consideration self-citations, or investigating citation and author networks.

For those with more technical abilities, a Google Scholar module has been written in Python that can be used as a command line tool or as part of a more extensive program (www.icir.org/christian/scholar.html).

Microsoft Academic Search

Google is not the only search engine with a bibliographic database. Microsoft has Microsoft Academic Search (http://academic.research.microsoft.com), and importantly it currently offers a set of APIs facilitating automated access to the data without researchers having to worry about finding themselves temporarily barred from services, although users wishing to make use of the APIs have to apply for an API key with details about how they wish to use the service.

Microsoft Academic Search also enables the browsing of content as well as searching. It allows users to browse the top-ranked authors, journals, publications, conferences, organizations and keywords within a particular research area. Unlike Google Scholar it has not been the focus of a large number of investigations, so there is little indication of the suitability of the robustness of the tool for bibliometric investigation. The Microsoft Academic Search API offers the sort of functionality that is currently missing in a tool like Publish or Perish, allowing not only access to the number of citations, but also the retrieval of the citing publications (Microsoft, 2012).

Additional tools

The web provides the opportunity for researchers to make use of new aggregators, to gather data from publishers themselves, and to adopt standards allowing for metadata to be harvested from institutional repositories. Such studies may include data that is not included within standardized bibliographic databases, for example metadata about figures and tables, as well as data from journals not included within a bibliographic database. It is important to recognize that the aims of journal publishers and the providers of bibliographic services are different, so while the bibliographic services need to monetize access to the metadata, publishers may promote a greater developer ecosystem in an attempt to drive traffic to the actual journal content.

Publishers provide a publisher-centric and journal-centric vision of the bibliographic ecosystem, whereas repositories offer a subject-centric and institutional-centric perspective, although the difference between the two is not always clear. arXiv.org is one of the more established repositories and provides an extensive API to its content (http://arxiv.org/help/api/index), and also a recognized resource in its own right. In Google Scholar's list of top publications seven areas of the arXiv.org repository are listed within its top 50 publications. There are now thousands of repositories for the hosting of preprints according to institution or for a particular subject area. As of June 2013, the OpenDOAR (www.opendoar.org) repository database listed 2336 repositories, most of which provide structured metadata according to the Open Archives Initiative Protocol for Metadata Harvesting (OAI-PMH). Many publishers also provide APIs for accessing their data, for example Springer (http://dev.springer.com) and Elsevier (www.developers.elsevier.com). The CrossRef Metadata Search (http://search.crossref.org/help/api) provides access to metadata from multiple publishers.

Although publishers and repositories provide a rich source of metadata for bibliographic investigations, it is an area that has been generally overlooked by the bibliometric community. This may in part be because there are not enough tools available for easily investigating these new resources. Greater interest is also likely to come as interacting with the publishers and repositories not only provides access to metadata, but may also increasingly facilitate access to the full text. For example, the PLoS API (http://api.plos.org) provides access to the metadata and all the text in articles, allowing for the search to be restricted to particular sections, e.g., introduction or results. As well as providing access to the metadata of over 5 million online documents, Springer also has an API providing access to the full text of over 80,000 Springer open access articles. Full text access is seen as an increasingly important part of resource discovery as data extraction tools help with the identification of concepts and relationships between articles, and may offer new insights into citation analysis (Bertin and Atanassova, 2012).

Despite the increase in bibliographic items included within the new bibliographic search engines, it is nonetheless important to recognize that they still do not index everything. There is still a wide range of documents that are not available online and each search engine is only indexing a selection of the web. This selection will depend heavily on the items it wants to include and how it identifies these items. We are still a long way from having an index of every bibliographic item that currently exists, let alone of every item that has ever existed.

Full text analysis

The term 'web metrics' is used throughout this book to refer to the quantitative measurement of the creation and use of web content. However, the distinction between web metrics and traditional bibliometrics is not always clear, especially with regards to the topic of web bibliometrics where the borders between the two are extremely blurred; whereas the use of Google Scholar may be considered a web metric tool, the Web of Science, which provides a similar service on the web, would be considered by most researchers to be primarily a traditional bibliometrics tool. There are obvious differences between the two in the quality of the data, access to the services and pre-web antecedents. This book takes a practical approach, focusing on those areas that would not have been possible offline, or at least would have been far more difficult offline. Full text analysis provides an example of investigations that would have been far more costly before the web, even if the content itself is not native to the web. For example, Silver (2012) shows how the frequency of use of the terms 'predictable' and 'unpredictable' changed over time through an analysis of the articles in the JSTOR digital library and in fiction books using Google Books Ngram Viewer (http://books.google.com/ngrams/info). At the beginning of the 20th century they were used with much the same frequency, then after the great depression and World War 2 unpredictable was used more than predictable, but during the latter part of the century predictable was used significantly more than unpredictable (see Figure 7.1). As both terms have finite, defined data sets, it would have been theoretically possible, although prohibitively expensive, to carry out the studies before the web came into existence. When there are millions of potential users of a service it is worthwhile carrying out the studies on the web.

The full text of documents offers much more than the opportunity to show the preponderance of certain terms over time: it enables natural language processing and data extraction techniques. From the perspective of traditional bibliometric investigations this may provide additional insights into citation analysis (Bertin and Atanassova, 2012), although the real hope is to find 'undiscovered public knowledge'.

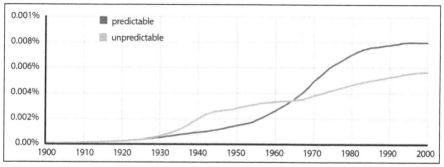

Figure 7.1 Use of the terms 'predictable' and 'unpredictable' in English books over the 20th century [Google and the Google logo are registered trademarks of Google Inc., used with permission]

The phrase 'undiscovered public knowledge' was coined by Swanson (1986) to describe knowledge that is in the public domain, but has not been found because increased specialization leads science to become ever more fragmented. The potential of automatic tools to help identify this knowledge is increasingly recognized, although while researchers may have the right to access journal articles for reading, they do not have the right to crawl the millions of articles that are available to identify new relationships (Van Noorden, 2013). Nevertheless text mining has formed the basis of ever more investigations, including some that have combined text mining with bibliometrics (e.g., He et al., 2012; Hung, 2012). There is a wide range of text mining tools available, both commercial (e.g., SAS Enterprise Miner and Leximancer) and open source (e.g., KNIME, http://tech.knime.org/knime-text-processing, and GATE, http://gate.ac.uk). While they are increasingly being adopted for research purposes, there is a tendency to point them at a set of data with little thought to their limitations, how they extract concepts, or whether they have been tested on data sets within a particular research domain.

The full text of traditional publications may also form the basis of research beyond science, through the mining of journal articles, and full text analysis of books enabled through projects such as Google Books. Although criticisms may be levelled at the quality of the digitizations, the limitations of optical character recognition and various rights issues, a project such as Google Books, with its stated aim of digitizing all books by 2020 (Jackson, 2010), undoubtedly offers a boon to digital research for those with the necessary skills and methodologies (Batke, 2010). Since Google Ngram Viewer was launched in 2010 an increasing number of studies have used it to investigate the appearance of words and phrases within the Google Books corpus. Twenge, Campbell and Gentile (2012b) have used it to investigate how male and female pronoun use in US books reflects women's status between 1900 and 2008, and the rise in individualistic words and phrases since the 1960s (Twenge, Campbell and Gentile, 2012a). Egnal (2013) has investigated the evolution of the American novel, comparing keywords in Ngram Viewer with a recently suggested framework for the evolution of the novel. Acerbi et al. (2013) explored the expression of emotions in 20th-century books, combining the ngrams from Google Books with the mood score from the lexical database WordNet (http://wordnet.princeton.edu) to explore emotional changes over the 20th century. Marriner and Morhange (2013) used Ngram Viewer to investigate the revival of catastrophism, which they found to be linked to an environmental awakening in the 1960s. Google Books is not the only resource, and there is an increasing number of other sources available for analysis. For example, Bode (2012) used AustLit (www.austlit.edu.au), the Australian literature resource, to gather insights into Australian literature as a whole rather than gaining insights from a few canonical texts.

Full text is undoubtedly useful for new areas of bibliometric research as it enables a wide range of investigations that would not have been possible a few years ago, and in the case of Google Ngrams makes a highly intuitive tool available to researchers in a wide range of disciplines. Although the web has facilitated the incorporation of additional bibliographic items and full text, it also provides space for the development of a far richer ecosystem around the bibliographic materials.

Greater context

Traditionally bibliometrics have provided rather limited insights into the use and impact of bibliographic materials. Although it might be argued that citations are the most important item for investigation because they are the strongest acknowledgement that one person's ideas are built on the ideas of others, it may be argued that for a long time citations were the most important item for bibliographic investigation because they were the only indicator of most scholarly outputs having any sort of impact! Although information about book sales and journal circulations would have been available to publishers, this would have provided a very limited perspective, because journal circulation is aggregated at the journal level rather than the article level, and libraries have such a vital role within the scholarly environment, with multiple users accessing the same volumes multiple times.

Although integrated library systems can now provide a host of information about the circulation of books and searches of the library catalogue, they are a very recent phenomenon in the history of scientific publishing, and even since the information has been available it has for the most part been housed within institutional silos. When journal articles only existed in paper copies on library shelves, there was generally nothing to indicate the number of times a journal article had been photocopied or read beyond the dog-earedness of a journal's pages.

In contrast, the web provides a wide range of insights into all types of bibliographic material, from information about the usage and holdings of bibliographic materials, to mentions of bibliographic materials on the web and social network sites.

Usage and holdings

Libraries and publishers continue to hold a lot of information about the use of bibliographic materials, and as the materials have been made available in a digital format so a greater range of data has become available.

As library catalogues and union catalogues such as the WorldCat (www.worldcat.org) and Copac (http://copac.ac.uk) are opened up to the web they provide an easily accessible source of information about library holdings. 'Libcitations' has been coined to refer to the appearance of a book in a national or international union catalogue (White et al., 2009). It could rightly be argued that libcitations are not a web metric in their truest sense. After all, the data is not being gathered from the web, but instead from databases that happen to have an interface on the web. However, libcitations are not as engrained within the library community as journal citations, and they were not routinely available in the pre-web era. Libcitations may be considered a particularly important resource about works that are no longer in print, and for which recent sales figures are no longer appropriate.

Library and information services are themselves also great generators of bibliometric information, and there have been a number of projects to highlight the potential of leveraging the power of the information held within library catalogues. The Jisc MOSAIC project in the UK has highlighted the potential of such data in the scholarly arena (http://ie-repository.jisc. ac.uk/466), noting that the University of Huddersfield had during a general period of downturn in book borrowing actually increased the number of titles borrowed per student, and the number of unique titles borrowed. Although there is undoubtedly a lot of potential information to be derived from catalogue data, the quantity of most data that is available to most libraries is far smaller than that available to a site such as Amazon, and will continue to be until there is a greater sharing of user data between libraries. Issues such as user confidentiality are likely to restrict access to vast quantities of library data from multiple institutions in the near future. Eventually, however, as institutions become more adept at aggregating user data, so that as with Google Trends individual behaviour is not discernible, it seems likely that increasing quantities of circulation data will become available. In 2012 Harvard Library announced that it would make the metadata for the 12 million items in its library freely available, and make the circulation data available in the future (Hardy, 2012).

The move towards digital publications has provided publishers with a wealth of information about usage, which has been described as essential if libraries are to know whether their electronic resources are being used effectively. This has led to the development of the Counting Online Usage of Networked Electronic Resource (COUNTER) to standardize how usage data is reported and Standardised Usage Statistics Harvesting Initiative (SUSHI) to facilitate the harvesting of this data (Pesch, 2007). Most of the major publishers are now COUNTER compliant, so access to the data provides new insights into the impact of content although, as Thelwall (2012) points out, there is still no guarantee that the work is actually being read.

Artificial inflation of usage figures may, to borrow the terminology of the search engine optimization community, be achieved through black hat or white hat means. Beel, Gipp and Wilde (2010) have emphasized the importance of academic search engine optimization, and while they argue that the idea is not to cheat the search engines, but rather help them, it would seem a fine line, and one that is all too easy to cross with researchers taking steps to inflate their figures by downloading their own content multiple times. While Edelman and Larkin (2009) found limited evidence of gaming the system for career reasons, they nonetheless found it to be driven by social comparisons; researchers were more likely to game the system when a download count increases visibility.

That users are likely to try and game a system that is inevitably open to abuse emphasizes the importance of having a battery of metrics, rather than relying on just one or two. This may be clearly seen in the PLOS ONE article 'An In-Depth Analysis of a Piece of Shit' (Krauth et al., 2012), which received 14,506 views and 10,516 shares in the first nine months of publication. That the title and the accompanying illustrations had some impact on the number of downloads would be hard to deny, and if they were taken in isolation this might result in an over-estimation of the work's scholarly impact. However, the additional metrics of the number of times the article has been cited and bookmarked are in keeping with expectations for similar articles.

User behaviour and user traces

As well as information from libraries and publishers, the web also enables the collection of a wide range of insights from other web users. As with evaluative investigations of impact on the web, web bibliometric investigations may focus either on user behaviour or the actual traces that people leave online.

Book sales – Amazon.co.uk

The most conclusive example of user behaviour that shows interest in a book is the actual buying of the book itself, and while online book stores may not provide access to user demographics their bestseller lists nonetheless demonstrate the areas that people are interested in. The vast size of online stores not only caters for the long tail of user needs, where a significant proportion of its sales comes from millions of volumes in small numbers (Anderson, 2006), but also provides a long tail of bestseller lists. Librarians are not restricted to keeping track of anything as broad as bestselling books, reference books, or even library and information science books; instead they could focus on an area as narrow as digital librarianship, or collection development. The way Amazon compiles its charts means that in areas where there are few sales the charts are fairly volatile, while many of the books may be inappropriately classified.

Google Trends

Web bibliometrics should not just revolve around the bestseller lists. Long after a book has fallen off the bestseller lists there may nonetheless be a lot of interest around a topic, and interest around a topic will not necessarily result in the buying of a book. Books, like any other subject, can be found among people's search activity, and like so many other subjects Google Trends (www.google.com/trends) can provide insights into the books people search for around the world through the Google search engine. Although in 2012 there was a lot of interest in E. L. James' *Fifty Shades of Grey*, 15 years after the first Harry Potter instalment was published Harry Potter books continued to be of greater interest that year (Figure 7.2).

The potential of Google Trends to provide insights into subjects such as

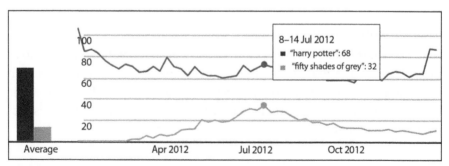

Figure 7.2 Harry Potter books vs Fifty Shades of Grey in Google Trends [Google and the Google logo are registered trademarks of Google Inc., used with permission]

books and authors has been recognized by Google, and it currently provides a top ten chart for a wide variety of topics including books and authors (www.google.co.uk/trends/topcharts). Although the charts are currently only formed from US data, it is possible to investigate how a term has been searched for around the world. While the Bible may not make it onto the Amazon bestseller chart very often, it has nonetheless dominated the Google Trends book chart since 2004, only once failing to be number one.

Google Trends can provide few insights, however, when it comes to the majority of bibliographic items, which will be searched for very rarely. For that it is necessary to investigate the traces that have been left on the web.

Web impact assessment

While Google Trends only provides aggregated search behaviour, search engines are designed to provide access to web pages however few results meet the criteria. A 'web impact assessment' is carried out when a search engine is used to investigate the appearance of particular terms and phrases, and one performs a 'web citation analysis' by using a web impact assessment to investigate the impact of academic articles (Thelwall, 2009). This may be thought of as taking a robust approach to the widespread habit people have of Googling themselves or their work. For example, it may be that someone wishes to investigate the relative impact of UK government research publications. This could be investigated by performing a phrase search for the titles of the publications through a search engine. Table 7.1 (overleaf) shows the findings of such a survey based on the first five research and analysis reports published in January 2012 on the GOV.UK website (www.gov.uk/government/publications) and investigated through Google Scholar and Google Search UK. Although Google Scholar has widened the realm of the types of document included within a bibliographic database, it has not indexed these particular items. That does not mean that the items will not have been mentioned within other documents, and indeed the two reports on HS2, a proposed high speed railway line, have indeed both been mentioned in three other reports. Google Scholar is only a sub-set of the documents that have been indexed by the Google search engine, and indeed we find that far more citing documents can be found. Two Google searches were carried out for each publication: first a phrase search in conjunction with *–site:gov.uk* to exclude those pages within the *gov.uk* domain, and second a phrase search with *filetype:pdf* to restrict the search to documents in a PDF format. Restricting the document type may be seen as restricting the search

Table 7.1 Web citation analysis of five UK government research publications in Google (July 2013)

Report title	Google Scholar	Google [-site:gov.uk]	Google [filetype:pdf-site:gov.uk]
'Participating in learning post-16: effective practice in schools'	Report not found	48	1
'Prize-driven innovation for development'	Report not found	57	1
'Regulatory co-operation and international trade'	Report not found	0	0
'Economic case for HS2: value for money statement'	3 cited reference searches	105	63
'Economic case for HS2 updated appraisal of transport user benefits and wider economic benefits'	3 cited reference searches	114	8

to those documents that are likely to be of higher quality.

As has been mentioned previously, the estimated number of search engine results identified on the first page of results is not as accurate as the estimated number of results when viewing the last accessible page of results. Table 7.1 shows the findings of a web citation analysis of five UK government research publications by going to the last accessible page of results, and including any similar pages originally omitted by Google.

From the initial analysis it seems clear that the HS2 documents have had the greatest impact by far, which is not unexpected as it is a very contentious project; whereas 'Regulatory co-operation and international trade' has not made any impact at all. While that may be sufficient for an initial analysis, where more robust findings are necessary it would be important to investigate the nature of the web citations through a content analysis to determine the nature of the citations (see Chapter 4).

Social network sites

Increasingly people are not creating and hosting their own web pages, but are making use of a large number of social network sites that ease the process of content creation. In many ways investigating the impact of a book is no different from monitoring the impact of any other topic. However, there are some social network sites that are likely to be of greater interest when looking into the impact of bibliographic items, and tools that have been built for gathering information from multiple sites and services.

Whereas citations are primarily of use in gaining insights into scholarly works, social network sites can now provide insights into works of every type. Amazon has now been joined by a host of social networks focused on books (e.g., Shelfari.com, LibraryThing and GoodReads) and thousands of reviews are available, instantly reduced to a number on a scale from one to five. While such book-focused social network sites can provide insights into some of the most popular books, so too can some of the more general social network sites such as Twitter. Even Wikipedia may be used to provide insights into people's views on some of the bestsellers.

Figure 7.3 compares the number of Wikipedia edits (collected 5 April 2013) with the number of books sold for 82 of the top 100 bestselling books of all time in the UK that were identified as having their own Wikipedia page, with the 100 bestselling books themselves being taken from the list on the *Guardian* Datablog (www.guardian.co.uk/news/datablog). The number of edits is shown on a logarithmic scale because of the power-law distribution editing in the number of edits that pages receive. When the Pearson correlation coefficient is calculated a statistically significant correlation ($p < 1\%$) is found between the number of edits a book's page receives and the number of books sold.

Although Figure 7.3 shows that there are a number of books with relatively heavily edited Wikipedia pages, despite not having a particularly high level of book sales, this may be a reflection of a particularly strong worldwide fan

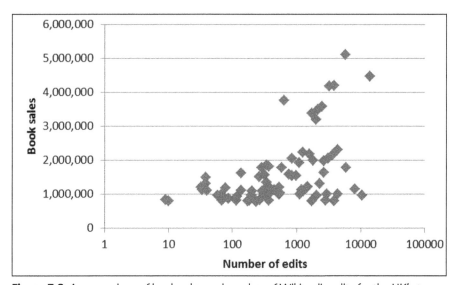

Figure 7.3 A comparison of book sales and number of Wikipedia edits for the UK's top selling books, April 2013

base and recent film tie-ins. For example, the second highest number of edits is for J. R. R. Tolkien's *Lord of the Rings*, despite selling the comparatively few 967,466 volumes in the UK since it was published.

While social network sites offer the potential to gain additional insights into books of all sorts, it is their potential to provide insights into the scholarly works that has gained the most interest, with the structured nature of social network content making it the foundation of altmetrics, using the structured nature of Web 2.0 technologies to establish alternative filters and indicators of research impact (Priem et al., 2010).

Many studies have now shown a link between online impact and the traditional impact as demonstrated through traditional citation measures. Eysenbach (2011) found Twitter mentions to be an early indicator of citations; Shuai, Pepe and Bollen (2012) found Twitter to be an indicator of downloads and citations; and Bar-Ilan et al. (2012) found a correlation between bookmarks on the academic social network Mendeley. These investigations have primarily been small scale, and focused on one metric. In a much larger investigation, investigating 11 different types of altmetric (including Twitter, LinkedIn, Google+ and Reddit mentions), Thelwall et al. (2013) found with the exception of Twitter that evidence was not prevalent enough to be useful in practice, although when sufficient evidence was available higher citations correlated with higher altmetrics.

Although altmetrics are unlikely to usurp citations' role in the near future, they are undoubtedly an area of growing interest, which is likely to grow in importance as researchers' working habits change, researchers can more easily be identified through projects such as ORCID (http://orcid.org), and data can be simply collected from across multiple sites at once (an issue that is returned to in the next chapter).

There are already a number of tools to help with the investigation of altmetrics, although the most extensive of these are commercial projects (e.g., www.plumanalytics.com, www.altmetric.com), and many publishers are increasingly using these services to promote the impact articles in their journals are having. Impact Story (http://impactstory.org) is a free service, however, which allows a researcher to build a profile of research outputs, and it then gathers information about the impact the outputs have had.

Conclusion

Within this chapter the discussion has revolved around the traditional scientific publications that continue to be such an important part of a researcher's work. As is increasingly recognized, the nature of publications is changing rapidly and librarians of the future will need to consider new ways of measuring their impact, and a far wider range of outputs than the linear text document that has formed the basis of academic output for hundreds of years.

For the foreseeable future, however, the established publications will continue to play a pivotal role in understanding the impact of researchers' work, and it seems as though alternative metrics will undoubtedly have a role to play. A battery of metrics is required showing the impact of different types of resources, in different ways, in different places.

8

Web metrics and the web of data

Introduction

Much of the discussion up to now has been about the potential of web metrics to gain insights into the web of documents: how many times has a particular document been mentioned on the web? How many times has a web page been visited? How many times has a wiki page been updated? It has been suggested, however, that we are moving from a web of documents to a web of data, where there is ever more data available in a machine-readable format. This chapter starts with a description of this 'web of data' and all its multiple facets, before expanding on the implications of this increasingly structured data on the development of various kinds of web metrics. Finally the chapter considers some of the existing tools for investigating this web of data.

The web of data

The term 'web of data' is used here to refer to data that is structured in machine-readable form and has been published openly on the web (Stuart, 2011). It is not separate from the existing web, but rather may refer to a subset of it, and includes a wide range of different technologies, from a Google spreadsheet hosted in the cloud, to an Excel spreadsheet contained within an institutional repository; from the APIs providing access to data from Web 2.0 sites and services, to web pages with microformats, microdata or Resource Description Framework in Attributes (RDFa). Some of these technologies have already been introduced during the book. Here we consider some of the technologies that contribute to the web of data in a bit more detail, considering both the advantages and disadvantages of the different technologies, before moving on to discuss some of the implications of the web of data (in its various guises) to the development of web metrics.

As has been argued elsewhere, librarians have a long history of providing access to the documents, and are ideally positioned for facilitating access to the increasingly large web of data (Stuart, 2011). Facilitating access to the web of data provides a new avenue for information services to develop as the traditional information services rapidly evolve. While the prospect of learning to program would understandably be a daunting prospect for many librarians, so-called massive open online courses (MOOCs) from sites such as Udacity (www.udacity.com) and Coursera (www.coursera.org) provide a simple way for librarians to expand their technical skills.

There is also a dynamic community of scrapers available at ScraperWiki (http://scraperwiki.com). The site provides a web-based platform where programmers can create code that is run automatically and the data is stored. Even if someone finds that the data has not already been scraped and they do not have the requisite skills to write the scraping program themselves, there is also the option to request data. You can pay someone to scrape the data for you.

From data documents...

The simplest way to contribute to the web of data is to place the data in a machine-readable format and upload it to the cloud or place it on a web server. The value of machine-readable formats can be observed when considering the difference between a PDF and an Excel spreadsheet; the PDF is a useful format for the human who wants to read or print a set of data, but less useful for the person who wants to reuse or experiment with the data. The publishing of data in machine-readable documents is increasingly widespread for two main reasons: the format enables a data document to be shared easily, and there is increasing recognition of the importance of open data.

Publishing a spreadsheet online has always been a relatively easy process for someone with a server space and an FTP client: it is no more difficult to upload a spreadsheet in an Excel or CSV format to a web server than it is to upload an HTML file or an image. There is an increasingly wide number of tools that make even the need for server space and an FTP client a thing of the past: a file may be uploaded to a service such as Google Drive then made publicly available to anyone who has the link; or the data can be uploaded to a site such as Many Eyes (www-958.ibm.com/software/analytics/manyeyes), which also allows for data visualization.

The biggest driver of the release of data is not necessarily technological, but rather the increased recognition of the potential of open data more generally. Organizations are recognizing the potential of open data to tap into the wisdom of the crowd; governments are responding to calls for greater transparency and recognizing the economic potential of their data; and the scientific community is recognizing the potential of open data to contribute to the progress of science. Data documents may not be the most efficient way to release this data, but it is a start and there is a wide range of innovative examples of publishing data online and reusing data that has been made publicly. The Guardian Datablog (www.guardian.co.uk/news/datablog) regularly publishes the data behind the news stories that it covers using tools such as Google spreadsheets to share data and ManyEyes to visualize it.

Like any other type of document, a data set can provide valuable insights into the way science is developing, and research has investigated the reuse of data sets through the established citation databases. For example, Piwowar, Carlson and Vision (2011) have begun tracking 1000 data sets from public repositories to see how they are referred to within the scholarly literature, although the authors acknowledge that such an approach overlooks other potential uses of the data, e.g., reuse by policy makers, within education, or for private study. Web citations may be available to provide a wider understanding, or usage information from a different perspective. As well as some scholarly data repositories that can provide usage statistics, governments have been among the big drivers of open data and the British Government data site (http://data.gov.uk/blog/site-usage) provides 'views' and 'downloads' for the site, different publishers (government departments) and individual data sets.

The real potential of the web of data for web metrics is not the analysis of data set usage, although this can undoubtedly provide interesting insights, but the large-scale analysis of the data itself. This is not facilitated by the data being shut away in silos, but by the data being shared on the web according to commonly agreed standards. This enables data to be read and understood from across the web without the need for a researcher to establish the idiosyncrasies in the structure of each particular data set.

...to the semantic web

The vision of a semantic web published in *Scientific American* in 2001 promised a future web where many of people's mundane computing tasks could be completed automatically by computer programs (Berners-Lee, Hendler and Lassila, 2001): booking an emergency appointment with a dentist; planning a holiday; identifying relevant documents; and retrieving specific answers to specific questions. Today such tasks generally continue to require a significant amount of human input beyond the mere formation of the query; even when booking a holiday, where a number of aggregators collect the information and draw it together in one place, we may visit multiple different aggregators before selecting the hotel we want.

Over a decade has passed since the semantic web gained widespread interest, and for most people's day to day activities the semantic web seems to have made little difference. During that time more standards that are necessary for the successful implementation of the semantic web (the so-called semantic web stack – http://en.wikipedia.org/wiki/Semantic_Web_Stack) have become established, and in recent years an increasing number of organizations have made data sets as Linked Data, from the British Museum catalogue to the Dewey Decimal Classification system and the Library of Congress Subject Headings. Linked Data emphasizes the importance of publishing data on the web in Resource Description Framework (RDF) triples, using Uniform resource identifiers (URIs) to represent things, and linking to other data sets (rather than making data available in an isolated fashion). As the standards become adopted, and agreed vocabularies emerge from communities across the web, far more extensive web metric investigations will be possible.

Building the semantic web

The core building block of the semantic web is the RDF triple, which forms a statement about a resource in the form of a subject–predicate–object triple. Such triples form meaningful data in isolation, but can also join together to make a large web graph. For example, each of the following triples is meaningful on its own:

- David [Subject] – Likes [Predicate] – Apples [Object].
- David – Likes – Oranges.
- Web Metrics for LIPs – has Author – David.
- Web Metrics for LIPs – has ISBN – 1856048748.

They also combine to make a larger web graph (see Figure 8.1).

Encoding these triples according to one of the recognized serializations of the RDF (i.e. structuring the data in a widely recognized machine-readable format) would enable these statements to be read by other computers.

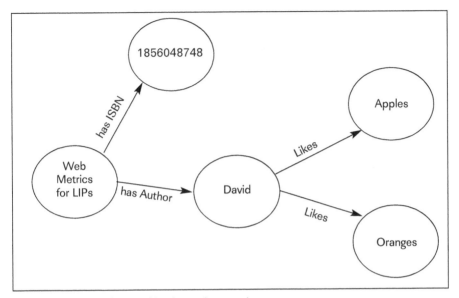

Figure 8.1 RDF triples combined as a data graph

However, these triples have a number of limitations, and could be improved: URIs have not been used to distinguish between similarly named objects; entities and their names have been combined; and widely adopted terminology has not been used.

URIs are unique strings of characters used to distinguish between resources on the web, the most well known of which are the URLs that web users enter in the address bar of their web browser to download the page they want to view. In the real world multiple people or objects may have the same name. For example, Apple may refer to the fruit, the computer company, or the record label. Making use of URIs prevents any ambiguity. In this case the Apple concept could be represented by a URI that already exists to represent the fruit in DBpedia: `http://dbpedia.org/resource/Apple`. Equally DBpedia can provide a URI to represent the orange fruit: `http://dbpedia.org/resource/Orange_(fruit)`. DBpedia (http://wiki.dbpedia.org) has extracted the structured information from Wikipedia and made it available as Linked Data; alternative URIs would also be available for representing Apple Records (`http://dbpedia.org/resource/Apple_Records`) and Apple the technology company (`http://dbpedia.org/resource/Apple_Inc.`), as well as orange the colour (`http://dbpedia.org/resource/Orange_(colour)`) and the telephone company (`http://dbpedia.org/resource/Orange_(telecommunications)`). The diverse nature of the content in Wikipedia means that DBpedia has URIs for a wide range of resources that individuals and organizations are likely to reference, so it plays an important role in linking diverse data sets across the linked open data cloud.

While DBpedia includes URIs for a wide range of resources, it by no means includes everything or everyone, but rather only those that reach Wikipedia's criteria of notability: `http://dbpedia.org/resource/David` does not represent the author of this book, but rather the biblical King David who is deemed to meet Wikipedia's guidelines of notability. Instead I may have chosen to create a Friend of a Friend (FOAF) personal profile on my own website so that I cannot only encode details about myself, but also represent myself, e.g., `www.davidstuart.co.uk/FOAF#me`. The #me identifier has been added so that it is possible to distinguish between the web page, and the person the URI is representing.

Although 'Web Metrics for Library and Information Professionals' may be considered quite a unique title for a book, it is quite possible (albeit highly unlikely) that someone else could write a similar book and give it the same title. It also confuses the title of the book with the book itself. Therefore it is important that the book is represented by a URI. The Open Library (http://openlibrary.org) has the stated aim of creating a single web page for every book, and provides this information in an RDF format so that it can be linked to by other RDF triples. Within the Open Library 'Web Metrics for Library and Information Professionals' is represented by the ID `http://openlibrary.org/books/OL25425715M`. The title may then be separated from the book.

In the first version the relationships between the different subjects and objects have been expressed in plain English, and a wide range of ontologies have been created for the encoding of certain types of relationship. For example, the FOAF ontology (which was briefly mentioned above) is an ontology for describing people and the relationships between them. The types of relationship expressed between the subjects and objects within this example are not unusual, and are already expressed in existing ontologies: Dublin Core (http://dublincore.org) has 'creator' and 'title' elements; the Bibliographic Ontology (http://bibliontology.com) may be used to express the ISBN; and while the term 'like' may have multiple meanings, the Facebook sense of 'liking' something may be expressed through the Citation Typing Ontology (CiTO; http://purl.org/spar/cito).

Making use of URLs and reusing existing ontologies produces a web graph that is meaningful to semantic web crawlers and agents (see Figure 8.2).

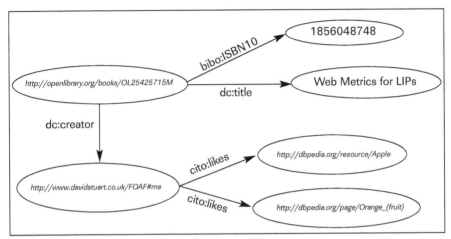

Figure 8.2 Data graph using URIs and shared ontologies

These triples can then be made available according to a number of widely adopted serializations. For example, a set of RDF triples about a book could be made available as RDF/XML:

```
<rdf:RDF
    xmlns:rdf="www.w3.org/1999/02/22-rdf-syntax-ns#"
    xmlns:dc="http://purl.org/dc/elements/1.1/">
    <rdf:Description
rdf:about="http://openlibrary.org/books/OL25425715M">
        <dc:title>Web metrics for LIPs<dc:title>
        <dc:creator>David Stuart</dc:creator>
    </rdf:Description>
</rdf:RDF>
```

In the Turtle (TTL – Terse Triple Language) format:

```
@prefix dc: <http://purl.org/dc/elements/1.1/>.
@prefix rdf: <www.w3.org/1999/02/22-rdf-syntax-ns#>.
<http://openlibrary.org/books/OL25425715M> dc:creator
"David Stuart";
        dc:title "Web metrics for LIPs".
```

Or as N-triples, which do not make use of compact URIs (CURIEs) and are therefore very accessible to the human reader:

```
<http://openlibrary.org/books/OL25425715M> <http://purl.
org/dc/elements/1.1/title>"WebmetricsforLIPs".
<http://openlibrary.org/books/OL254257I5M> <http://purl.
org/dc/elements/1.1/creator>"DavidStuart".
```

The N-triple serialization has also been extended to form N-quads, so that information may be collected about the triple and its context – where the triple was found.

Such serializations may either be created on the fly as a particular request is made of a triple store (a database specifically designed for the storing of triples), or the RDF may be encoded within a text file that is stored in a particular location.

Linked Data has been described as the semantic web done right, and has given added impetus to the semantic web; there have been a number of semantic web projects in recent years. However a more semantic web does not have to be about the creation of large databases or content or the encoding of separate semantic web files. In fact a widely adopted semantic web is most likely to come about through being incorporated into the current web.

Embedded semantics

There are a number of different approaches to incorporating semantic content into existing HTML, and three of the most important ones are briefly discussed here: RDFa, microformats and microdata. These are not the only attempts that have been made to embed semantic information within web pages. For example, embedded RDF (eRDF) was an alternative (now obsolete) method of embedded RDF within HTML, while ContextObjects in Spans (COinS) is a method to embed bibliographic metadata within HTML that emerged from within the library community. RDFa, microformats and microdata are, however, the most important: RDFa because of its close relationship to Linked Data; microformats because they have been so widely adopted; and microdata because it is not only native to HTML5, but has gathered significant interest from the major search engines.

RDFa

RDFa is a means of encoding full RDF within HTML web pages. Originally this was restricted to XHTML, although the latest iteration is suitable for HTML as well (W3C, 2012a). The creation of RDFa content does not appear more user-friendly than the creation of standard RDF:

```
<div xmlns:dc="http://purl.org/dc/elements/1.1/"
   about=" http://openlibrary.org/books/OL25425715M">
   <span property="dc:title">Web metrics for LIPs</span>
   <span property="dc:creator">David Stuart</span>
</div>
```

The key difference is that it is not necessary to create separate content, but rather content management systems can be created to add mark-up to the normal web pages that are to be published.

Microformats and microdata

It could be argued that the RDF triple is overly complex in most instances, and even RDF is not particularly user-friendly. It is important to recognize that, while Linked Data has garnered a lot of interest in recent years, it is not the only approach to creating a more semantic web. Microformats have been very successful, claiming over 70% of structured data on web pages to be in a microformat standard (Microformats, 2012). Microformats are not an overarching framework designed to incorporate every eventuality like RDF, but rather attempt to solve specific problems, making use of the existing capabilities of HTML, according to the principle of being designed for people first and machines second.

Microformats provide a limited number of stable and draft formats for some of the most commonly used content, for example, hCalendar for encoding information about events, hCard for encoding contact information, and hReview for reviews and ratings. One of the principles of microformats is that all data that is encoded should be visible on a web page to encourage the data to be kept up to date, and to dissuade people from trying to manipulate the structured data to encourage more traffic. By focusing on a small number of standards, microformats provide the 'low lying fruit' of a semantic web (Singer, 2009).

While RDFa enables the full expressivity of the semantic web, and microformats provide the majority of semantic content on the web today, the rapidly emerging format is microdata. Microdata is native to HTML5, and may be viewed as lying half-way between RDFa and microformats. It aims for the simplicity of microformats through the use of name–value pairs, while not being restricted to a small number of universally agreed vocabularies.

Implications of the web of data for web metrics

It is not entirely clear which vision of the web of data will dominate: the continuation of data silos or a more integrated semantic web: a semantic web embedded within HTML or one existing alongside the existing web of documents; RDF triple or name–object pairs. Even in its most limited of forms the web of data offers a boon to the establishment of web metrics through an increase in the availability of public data that may be analysed and compared with other data sets. However, such documents are still likely to require a significant amount of effort by a researcher to make use of the data. It seems clear that we are also inching towards an increasingly semantic web, and whichever form this takes it has important implications for the development of new web metrics.

The lack of widely adopted standards has meant that until now most web metric investigations have either focused on data from a small part of the web, such as data from one particular social networking site, or have had to draw conclusions about the meaning of a high web impact or relationships expressed through web links through correlations and content analysis. In comparison an increasingly semantic web enables the investigation of structured content across multiple websites, where even the reasons for link placement can potentially be made explicit. A semantic web offers the potential for insights across all areas of web metrics.

Standardization in the way that data is structured is becoming increasingly widespread, as are many of the ontologies, which may be defined as 'formal, explicit specification of a shared conceptualisation' (Gruber, 1993). Librarians have been at the centre of the development of many semantic web ontologies, and it is not surprising therefore to find bibliographic data being one of the areas with the most established ontologies. As well as the long established Dublin Core (http://dublincore.org), which is designed to describe a wide range of web resources, there are specialized ontologies for bibliographic materials (e.g., The Bibliographic Ontology; http://bibliontology.com) and ontologies for aggregating resources (e.g., Open Archives Initiative – Object Reuse and Exchange; www.openarchives.org/ore/). There is even an ontology for that most common bibliometric unit of analysis: the citation. The CiTO enables the expression of a wide range of reasons that one paper might be cited by another, e.g., 'agrees with', 'cites as recommended reading', 'disputes'. The widespread use of the CiTO ontology would inevitably enable more refined citation analysis, and refute some of the criticisms that have previously been made about citation analysis. The CiTO ontology has been incorporated into CiteULike (www.citeulike.org), the social bookmarking service for academic papers, enabling users to express CiTO relationships between papers. The semantic web also offers the opportunity for criticism and discussion around articles that are not reflected in the scholarly literature. Too often it has been suggested that journals are reluctant to follow up the publication of papers with publications of the criticisms of those papers; a semantic web would enable such discourse to be easily identifiable. A semantic web also offers the potential for the improved information retrieval of resources, a fact which is reflected in the support of four major search engines (Google, Bing, Yahoo and Yandex) for Schema.org, a shared mark-up vocabulary for expressing web content using microdata or RDFa.

The semantic web also offers the potential for far more detailed investigations into the processes of science, especially as increasing amounts of scientific activity and discourse takes place online. Even something as simple as bookmarking and making notes about online resources could make use of the Open Annotation Ontology (www.openannotation.org), while at the other extreme some scientific disciplines have developed a whole ontological framework. Understanding and opening up the research would allow for not only the development of new tools to meet researchers' needs, but also building on one another's work. While researchers may not wish to share all their data, especially their notes, even something as impersonal as the highlighting of text may save the time of other researchers in finding the most relevant parts of a text.

There would seem to be no area for webometric investigation that could not be enhanced by the widespread adoption of semantic web ontologies. In the same way that citation analysis could benefit from the widespread adoption of an ontology such as CiTO, such an ontology (or a more specialized version) would also be used for hyperlink analysis. Social networks analysis could also be enabled across multiple sites through the use of ontologies such as FOAF, rather than the idiosyncratic proprietary formats. While a widespread linking ontology would be useful for large-scale webometric analysis, it would also help web analytics, enabling a quick method for gathering feedback on sites and services.

For now, however, the problem is that very few of the ontologies have been widely implemented. This may partly be because of the difficulty in identifying appropriate ontologies, something that has been likened to dowsing rather than a scientific selection of appropriate ontologies (W3C, 2012a); although it may be possible to determine whether an ontology has gone sufficiently mainstream when it has been incorporated within Schema.org, this does not necessarily identify the most appropriate ontology for a particular task. The requirements of individuals wishing to mark up their web page so their friends can find their online content are likely to be different from the requirements of a research group wanting to encode details about researchers and their work; whereas FOAF may be suitable for one, the Common European Research Information Format (CERIF) may be more suitable for the other. Understanding the ontologies that are available within a particular field and how they have been adopted is likely to become an increasingly important part of librarians' work. Although within some fields there are websites that provide well developed ontology libraries, e.g., BioPortal (http://bioportal.bioontology.org) for the biomedical community, in many areas the identification of appropriate ontologies continues to be an arduous process.

Investigating the web of data today

It is still very much the early stages in the development of tools for investigating the semantic web. Many of those tools that have been developed have emerged from the academic sector, and they have often been associated with a short-term project. Nevertheless, some of the tools that are available provide much greater functionality than is currently available on traditional web search engines, and have the advantage of being designed with the automated user in mind.

As with an investigation of web documents, the suitability of one tool over another depends heavily on the nature of the investigation, and the type of data that librarians are interested in. If the researcher is only interested in the data set of one or two sites, it may be that a SPARQL endpoint is available, allowing the simple querying of the data. Larger investigations may require the use of a web crawler or a third-party service such as Sindice, which indexes the semantic web.

SPARQL

SPARQL, pronounced 'sparkle', is an RDF query language, in which the user represents the graph pattern they wish to match. Graph patterns are like RDF triples, but each part of the triple may also be a variable, to represent the unknown aspect of the triple. For example, if users wanted to find a book with a particular ISBN, they might wish to match the graph pattern:

```
?book bibo:isbn13 "9781856047456"
```

In this case ?book is a variable used to represent a URI of the book, which is unknown, and "9781856047456" is the ISBN of the book. The predicate bibo:isbn13 requires knowledge of the particular ontologies that are used in a triple store, in this case the Bibliographic Ontology introduced earlier, which forms part of the data model for the Linked Data version of the British National Biography. Querying the British National Biography may be achieved by entering the appropriate query in the British Library's SPARQL editor – http://bnb.data.bl.uk/flint:

```
PREFIX bibo: <http://purl.org/ontology/bibo/>
SELECT ?book
WHERE {
    ?book bibo:isbn13 "9781856047456".
}
```

The query above has three parts: PREFIX allows for the use of abbreviations in the use of URIs; SELECT informs the database which variables are to be returned; and WHERE provides details of the pattern that the graph should be matched against. As there is only one book with any particular ISBN, entering the query would find one ?book result, <http://bnb.data.bl.uk/id/resource/015855235>, the URI representing the book. To retrieve additional details requires a more extensive query:

```
PREFIX bibo: <http://purl.org/ontology/bibo/>
PREFIX dct: <http://purl.org/dc/terms/>
PREFIX foaf: <http://xmlns.com/foaf/0.1/>
SELECT ?authorname ?title

WHERE {
    ?book bibo:isbn13 "9781856047456";
          dct:creator ?authorURI;
          dct:title ?title.
    ?authorURI foaf:name ?authorname.
}
```

This query matches books that not only have the particular ISBN, but where the book also has a title and a creator, and the creator has a name. If any of this information was not available, then no results would be returned. However, SPARQL also allows OPTIONAL graph pattern matching so the additional information would be returned if it was available, but it would not prevent the retrieval of the results if the data was not available.

In the above example only one result was found, although for many queries there are multiple results. For example, it is possible to request every FOAF name in a triple store with a ?subject foaf:name ?object graph pattern, or even to request all triples irrespective of predicate:

```
SELECT ?subject ?predicate ?object
WHERE {
  ?subject ?predicate ?object
}
LIMIT 50
```

In many cases the triple store has a maximum number of results it will provide, or will time-out if the query is too broad. Where a broad query is being used to explore the nature of the terminology used within a triple store, it is best to limit the number of results by adding a LIMIT to the end of the query.

With the increased interest in Linked Data in recent years, a large number of Linked Data data sets have been published with SPARQL front ends so users may enter their query through a web browser as well as by sending queries automatically. As well as the British Library's British National Bibliography (http://bnb.data.bl.uk/flint), a few other large data stores with SPARQL front ends that are likely to be of interest to librarians include:

- DBpedia (http://dbpedia.org/sparql), which has extracted the structural data from Wikipedia, and therefore covers data from a wide range of topics
- the British Museum Collection Data (http://collection.britishmuseum.org/Sparql)
- Data.gov (http://services.data.gov/sparql)
- Data.gov.uk (http://data.gov.uk/sparql)
- Nature Linked Data Platform (http://data.nature.com).

Many of these sites may provide large enough collections in their own right for investigation: has the age at which authors publish their first book changed over the last century? What are the growth areas of the British Museum collection? Although the real value of the semantic web metrics, like web metrics more generally, comes from the analysis of data across multiple sites.

Sindice

Although a number of semantic web search engines and other indexing tools have been developed, most of these have been developed within the academic community in conjunction with relatively short-term projects, and it is not always clear to what extent they are still gathering data or whether the full functionality is still being offered. Probably the most extensive of the semantic web indexers that is active and being actively developed is Sindice (http://sindice.com). It indexes not only RDF, but also microformats, microdata and RDFa. In summer 2013 it claimed to have indexed 708.19 million documents, which equate to billions of triples. Most importantly it has a wide range of interfaces for querying the data. As well as simple and advance search interfaces, it provides an extensive API and has a SPARQL endpoint, and most recently incorporated an analytics tool to provide insights into the ontologies used within specific domains, and the domains on which an ontology is popular.

As with earlier web metric investigations making use of traditional search engines, Sindice does not always provide the results that are expected, or the functionality that may be required. For example, Stuart (2012) investigated the use of the FOAF ontology within the UK academic web space. Although this should, theoretically, have been possible by sending multiple queries to the SPARQL endpoint, in fact the endpoint kept timing out. It was therefore necessary to search for use of the FOAF:name predicate in the .uk domain, and then filter the results according to whether the results also included the 'ac' in the URL. This provided a sufficiently small set of documents that could then be downloaded, and automatically checked that they were indeed from the .ac.uk second or top-level domain, and that the 'ac' had not appeared elsewhere in the URL.

Nevertheless, such a service provides quick access to data from (and across) multiple domains, and generally more data than most researchers would be able to gather for themselves. For example, Table 8.1 (overleaf) provides details of the structured data on the main domain of the Russell Group universities as seen through the analytics service (http://demo.sindice. net/dataset/). In the same way that the Webometrics.info rankings of

Table 8.1 Structured content at Russell Group universities indexed by Sindice (July 2013)

University	URL	Pages with structured data	Total number of triples
University of Birmingham	www.birmingham.ac.uk/	0	0
University of Bristol	www.bristol.ac.uk/	9	2.39k
University of Cambridge	www.cam.ac.uk/	505	7.61k
Cardiff University	www.cardiff.ac.uk/	1	10
Durham University	www.dur.ac.uk/	6	74
University of Edinburgh	www.ed.ac.uk/home	685	14.24k
University of Exeter	www.ex.ac.uk/	0	0
University of Glasgow	www.gla.ac.uk/	18	123
Imperial College London	www3.imperial.ac.uk/	0	0
King's College London	www.kcl.ac.uk/	62	680
University of Leeds	www.leeds.ac.uk/	286	2.26k
University of Liverpool	www.liv.ac.uk/	6	173
London School of Economics & Political Science	www.lse.ac.uk/	176	848
University of Manchester	www.manchester.ac.uk/	212	2.61k
Newcastle University	www.ncl.ac.uk/	311	36.90k
University of Nottingham	www.nottingham.ac.uk/	16	439
University of Oxford	www.ox.ac.uk/	8.31k	229.86k
Queen Mary, University of London	www.qmul.ac.uk/	0	0
Queen's University Belfast	www.qub.ac.uk/	0	0
University of Sheffield	www.sheffield.ac.uk/	0	0
University of Southampton	www.soton.ac.uk/	11.58k	402.63k
University College London	www.ucl.ac.uk/	104	7.90k
University of Warwick	www2.warwick.ac.uk/	3	440
University of York	www.york.ac.uk/	7.53k	248.22k

universities and repositories considers openness to be a key aspect of an organization's web presence, and incorporates the number of rich files (e.g., .pdf and .doc) indexed by Google Scholar into its rankings, the amount of structured content may also be considered an increasingly important aspect of a site's presence.

As can be seen, there is a wide variation in the amount of structured content each of the sites has. At one extreme there are many sites which continue to have no triples, while at the other extreme the University of Southampton has over 400,000 indexed triples. As with data collected through traditional search engines, it is important to distinguish between reality, and the picture of reality as operationalized through particular tools.

Although there has not been the same scrutiny of semantic web metric tools that has been applied to traditional web metric tools, the limitations of the tools can already be seen. For example, although Sindice reports Queen's University Belfast has no pages with structured data, and consequently no triples, it nevertheless reports the contradictory information that the most popular classes used on qub.ac.uk are vCard properties. Equally, the information about the popularity of a class on a particular website may differ according to the perspective of the query. For example, at the time of writing, the domain that makes most use of the EPrint class (http://eprints.org/ontology/EPrint) is the University of Southampton with a cardinality of 8.90 thousand, while the EPrint class is the most used class on the University of Southampton site with a cardinality of 8.71 thousand.

Nevertheless such tools offer the potential for a wide range of semi-evaluative indicators. As with the web of documents, if greater knowledge is required about which data has been crawled and the reasons for potential discrepancies when querying the data, researchers may need to gather the data for themselves.

LDSpider – an RDF web crawler

Just as there are web crawlers for the web, so are there web crawlers for the web of data. Some are designed purely for RDF (e.g., LD Spider; http://code.google.com/p/ldspider), while others allow for the extraction of a far wider range of data including RDFa, Microformats and Microdata (e.g., Anything to Triples – http://any23.apache.org – the crawler behind the Sindice website).

In some ways crawling the web of data is far simpler than crawling the traditional web. The data is designed to be collected and analysed automatically, although this means that tool development is primarily the preserve of computer scientists rather than being designed for regular users, and investigating the web of data can require cobbling together a number of different pieces of code, and user interfaces are often of the non-graphical variety. Nevertheless the tools are readily available for those with slightly more technical skills, and the patience to string together a number of different tools, to quickly collect a large amount of data from the semantic web.

For example, LDSpider (http://code.google.com/p/ldspider) may either be integrated into a larger computer program, or run from the command prompt once it has been downloaded. It allows for the creation of a seedlist from which to start the crawl, different crawling strategies (breadth-first or load balancing), and the following of only certain predicates in the identification of additional documents (e.g., only following FOAF:knows relationships). Once the LDSpider jar file has been downloaded from the website, and with the command prompt directory changed to the same one as the jar file, the following line will run the crawler with a breadth-first crawl, taking a seed list from the seed.txt file and outputting the results to a text file called breadth.nq in the same folder:

```
java -jar ldspider-1.1e.jar –b 50 10 –f http://xmlns.com/foaf/0.1/knows -s
seed.txt -o breadth.nq
```

Making use of the jar file programmatically allows the data to be exported in a number of serializations, and the command prompt only outputs the RDF in the N-Quad serialization. Although this is one of the more user-friendly RDF serializations, showing both the triple and the URL at which it was found, N-Quads are one of the newer serializations, and not all analysis software can deal with it. The data needs to be transformed, something that can be done with any23 or through the downloading of an additional piece of software, e.g., RDFconvert (http://sourceforge.net/projects/rdfconvert). Once the data is in the RDF/XML serialization it may be analysed with a wide range of software. For example, it could be explored through RDF Gravity (http://semweb. salzburgresearch.at/apps/rdf-gravity); an RDF graph visualization tool, Twinkle (www.ldodds.com/projects/twinkle), may be used to carry out SPARQL investigations of the data; while the semantic web plug-in for Gephi (http:// wiki.gephi.org/index.php/SemanticWebImport) enables the data to be queried, visualized and subjected to established social network analysis methodologies.

Figure 8.3 shows FOAF network based on data collected through the LDSpider using the crawl parameters mentioned above and using Tim Berners-Lee's FOAF page (http://dig.csail.mit.edu/2008/webdav/timbl/foaf.rdf) as the starting point. As the crawler downloads whole documents that are linked to by FOAF:name, and not just those triples within the document that include the predicate FOAF:name, it is necessary to include a SPARQL query so that only the FOAF graph is displayed/analysed:

```
construct { ?x <http://xmlns.com/foaf/0.1/knows>   ? y}
where { ?x <http://xmlns.com/foaf/0.1/knows> ? y}
```

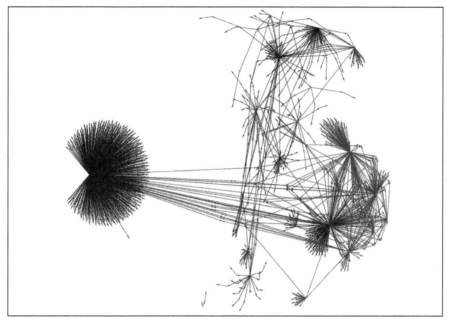

Figure 8.3 Graph for a FOAF network discovered through an LDSpider crawl

Such a graph may then be subjected to the same types of social network analysis discussed in Chapter 6, investigating concepts such as centrality and clustering.

Conclusion

Only time will tell to what extent semantic web technologies will be adopted, although they have the potential to be a boon for web metric investigations, breaking down the current research silos, and allowing a host of detailed cross site analysis. For this to happen it is necessary for librarians to become increasingly involved in the identification of existing ontologies and the development of new ontologies.

Although the technologies are not as seamless or intuitive as those that may form the basis of social network analysis or even web link analysis, as this chapter has shown there is a large quantity of data available for those willing to take the time to learn about the new technologies.

9

The future of web metrics and the library and information professional

Whenever you can, count.

Sir Francis Galton (1884)

By this stage of the book it is to be hoped that librarians will have been persuaded about the potential for web metrics in their professional activities. Even if they are not quite ready to start advertising a web metric service to their users, they will at least recognize the importance of tracking their own metrics, and should be dissuaded from merely reaching for the closest numbers to hand.

This last chapter considers the potential future of web metrics and its relationship with librarians. As has been emphasized throughout this book new web technologies are frequently emerging, and so are the tools available to investigate them. It would be a fool's errand to attempt to predict the emergence of any specific new technology or tool, or the future dominance of any particular website, but it is reasonable to expect certain current trends to continue, such as the digitization of analogue content and the capturing of an increased amount of data from our daily lives. It may also be expected that much of this data will increasingly be open, although this is by no means definite. While some embrace the opportunities for new services that are offered by the sharing of information, others are concerned about the seemingly inevitable loss of privacy that comes with it. Each of these changes will have potential ramifications for web metrics and how they can be used by librarians.

Before we hurtle towards the future it is important to pause for a moment and reflect on how far we have come, not only in this book, but with web metrics.

How far we have come

As would be expected of a book called *Web Metrics for Library and Information Professionals*, this book has discussed a wide range of tools and sources. These have included: web crawlers, semantic web crawlers, social network sites, RDF triples, APIs, data extractors, data scrapers, data aggregators and graph visualization software. The full list would be a long one, and as we necessarily move rapidly from one technology to another, it is easy to overlook the scale of what is being discussed. After all, it is not unreasonable to liken the development of web crawlers and services such as Google Trends to early examples of scientific instruments that provided insights into the physical world.

When Robert Hooke's *Micrographia* was published in 1665 he created the world's first scientific bestseller. His modified microscope allowed him to create intricate drawings of objects whose finer details had largely been unseen, although the objects themselves were familiar to 17th-century gentlemen. Hooke's drawings included fleas, lice, nettle stings and even crystals of frozen urine, and he is credited with increasing interest in microscopy more widely. As has been demonstrated in this book, web metric tools can also be used to provide novel insights into a world that is in many ways familiar, although there has yet to be a *Micrographia*-like work that has captured the public's imagination to the same extent. In fact in a world where endless innovation seems normal, tools are assimilated with barely a second glance as the public waits to be enticed by the next shiny tool on the horizon. Google Trends, a service which enables people to have insights into the accumulated thoughts of hundreds of millions of people around the whole, is not only accepted as normal but is liable to draw complaints that the data is not accessible automatically, or that it does not provide a fine enough level of granularity.

The web metric tools of the future will undoubtedly be better, and enable a far wider range of analysis than is currently possible, but we should not forget how far we have come already, and the potential of the tools that are currently available.

The future of web metrics

More data

Nothing about the future is ever certain, but short of the decline of civilization itself, it would seem safe to predict that the web will continue to grow, and with it the potential for web metric investigations. There is now an ever increasing quantity of data that is being made available online by a wide range of individuals and organizations. There is a large number of causes for the increase in the data that is available, of which four are briefly considered here: the digitization of analogue content, working in the cloud, the web of things, and the development of new scientific tools.

It could be argued that large-scale digitization projects receive a disproportionately large amount of attention in comparison with the quantity of information that is being placed online and the proportion of analogue information that has actually been digitized. Although Google Books has digitized over 30 million volumes this has now been dwarfed by the amount of social media content that has been created and continues to be created, while books are only a very small proportion of information that is held in libraries, archives, museums and galleries around the world. In many instances this information continues to exist only in a physical form, and not even digital versions of the metadata are available. Nevertheless the ongoing digitization of analogue content facilitates the potential to carry out a greater variety of work online.

An increasing number of activities in our professional and personal lives occur online, and this looks set to increase as more specialized services and infrastructures are developed for the accomplishment of a wider range of tasks. Such services and infrastructures provide new information sources as people create and publish content, and there is also the potential for a wide range of paradata – the sub-set of metadata that is not fixed, such as usage statistics – although it seems likely that paradata will become ever more sophisticated.

The creation of data is not restricted to deliberate content creation by people, but may also be created automatically as we move closer towards a web of things, and objects in the real world are connected and share information over the web. Most people already carry mobile phones everywhere they go, allowing for a wide range of location-based services, while smart meters are increasingly being installed that automatically share information about energy consumption. These smart meters can potentially provide a wide range of information about people's habits: how they spend their leisure time, how often they go away, and when they have guests. There are already a wide range of web enabled sensors, sharing information about air quality (e.g., http://airqualityegg.com), reminding people to water their plants (www.koubachi.com), as well as wi-fi biosensors for monitoring people's blood pressure, heart rates and sugar levels. It can be expected that as prices fall such products will become more widely adopted, and the range of products available will also increase.

Domestic sensors are by no means the only creators of vast quantities of data. Vast quantities of data are being collected as ever more sophisticated scientific tools are developed. From the Large Hadron Collider to DNA sequencers, the world is now awash with data. It is not yet clear how much of this data will be made publicly available.

More open

In recent years there has been a big push towards making non-personal information from the public sector publicly available. This includes greater sharing of the data that government collects, on how it spends public finances, and from public funded research. The open sharing of much of the data that can be shared relies not on the decisions of governments or large corporations but on individuals. While research councils may require that the data produced in a research project is made publicly available, they are unlikely to insist that as a researcher makes use of online resources and tools, paradata about their activities is also shared. Equally, while households may be willing to have smart meters fitted to aid in the collection of information about energy use, privacy advocates are concerned about the regularity with which energy companies collect this highly sensitive data (which enables them to begin building knowledge of people's behaviour) and are unlikely to recommend the public sharing of such data.

Yet, as is regularly discovered in surveys of personal data published online, there are large portions of the population who are willing to share a lot of personal information publicly. In fact, with some people there is the problem that they overshare as the distinctions between private and public spaces become confused (Agger, 2012). What has been seen is that most people are willing to share personal information when there is a perceived benefit, especially if the default is in favour of the public sharing of information.

Whereas the public sharing of profile information may benefit a user through the accumulation of social capital, different user groups are likely to require different incentives for the sharing of different types of information and for different communities of users. Generally the sharing of data from a person's smart meter is unlikely to do much for their social capital, but if by sharing the information other people identified ways that they could save money, a person might be willing to do so. Equally, while a researcher may be reluctant to share much of the content that they create online, they may be more willing to do so if they recognize that useful tools and services can be built on this data.

It also seems likely that current attitudes to privacy will change as those who make the decisions have been born into a world where the web has always existed, and where they will have always shared certain information publicly.

More web metrics

Although an increase in the amount of data available for analysis would inevitably provide the potential for a large number of new web metric studies, it could also be argued that we are already at the stage where there is more than enough data freely available for analysis; we just need the tools, methods and people to ask the right questions.

As has already been seen, a wide range of tools has been developed over the years for the collection of web data, but there is still a lot to do to develop tools that can make the best use of the data that is available. There is a need to develop more open tools to make use of the data that is available, not merely relying on the data that is available through the APIs of search engines and social network sites, and making use of the functionality that is given rather than that may actually be wanted. In this age of big data there will also be new challenges relating to the tools and methodologies required for the indexing and analysing of the new quantities of data that are available.

New approaches will also be required to deal with the influx of new data types that may become the focus of investigations. For example, as vast quantities of code become available it may be that automatic analysis of the code can help identify code that is well written, as well as give insights into a bricolage approach to the sharing of code. The identification of quality code will not be as simple, but as with Dijkstra's (1968) case against the GO TO statement in the structure of early programming, hard rules may be identified for distinguishing the quality of code.

The biggest change, however, is likely to be in the growing importance of metrics and data analysis. Data scientists have been described in *Harvard Business Review* as having the sexiest job of the 21st century (Davenport and Patil, 2012), and whereas data science brings together hacking skills, statistical skills and domain expertise in the business setting to provide novel insights, and the e-scientist does something similar in the scientific area, web metrics is about focusing these skills on the most important source of information in the 21st century, the web. There is now increased interest in the potential of metrics in a host of fields that may previously have given more attention to gut feelings, most famously recounted for the worlds of baseball and football in the bestsellers *Moneyball* (Lewis, 2004) and *Soccernomics* (Kuper and Szymanski, 2012).

The future of the library and information professional and web metrics

Throughout, this book has tried to emphasize the application of web metrics in a wide number of areas that are likely to be of interest to librarians in many situations. The question that naturally arises from this is whether it should be expected that librarians include the application of web metrics into their existing roles or if it requires distinct posts to be established.

Like many areas of expertise within the library profession, the answer would seem to be that while it is useful for everyone to have a passing acquaintance with the basics of web metrics, there is nonetheless a need to also have a specialized skill level. This is equally true of other areas within the information profession, e.g., bibliometrics, cataloguing and classification. Although it may be useful for everyone in the library profession to have a general understanding of some of the tools that are available and the research that can be accomplished, they do not necessary all need to have a high level of expertise in data collection and manipulation, or the statistical tests necessary to draw any inferences.

Even within the realm of web metrics there is liable to be a number of areas where the specialization of more than one person is useful; a web analytics report into the impact of a library's social media presence requires a very different set of skills from a semantic web scientometric investigation into the ontologies that are being used within a particular field. Whether specialists are required within specific areas will depend not only on the size of the library, but also on the future of the different areas of web metrics.

Web analytics

Web analytics differs from the other areas of web metrics discussed in this book in that rather than a service that librarians are likely to offer to library users, it focuses on the impact of the library itself. The implementation of performance indicators within a library is not new, and there are already internationally recognized standards such as ISO 11620: 2008 Information and Documentation – Library Performance Indicators. However, when it comes to content on the web it becomes especially important as in a fast changing environment it is necessary to understand how best to make use of services, if indeed the library should be bothering with a service at all.

The exact nature of web analytics inevitably reflects the emergence of new sites and services, the development of new technologies designed to track user behaviour, as well as changes to information privacy laws. Nonetheless it seems likely that the importance of web analysis will gain wider recognition, and within large organizations web analytic positions are likely to become centralized or outsourced to dedicated web analytics firms. It is important, however, that librarians at least keep a passing interest in their own metrics. The aims and objectives of social media or web content cannot be simply reduced to receiving the most hits or the most followers, and it is only by understanding the context of the particular content that the metrics are really meaningful.

One of the most important aspects of web analytics is that it is a useful tool for the promotion of metrics more widely. Although informetrics has always had the potential to be a useful part of a librarian's work, the methodologies have not been widely adopted in practice. Web analytics can demonstrate the potential of metrics to librarians and a library's users.

Bibliometrics, scientometrics and altmetrics

The areas of web metrics that align most closely with the current practices of a librarian are those associated with bibliometrics, scientometrics and altmetrics. As existing publications evolve and new publishing genres emerge, it will become increasingly meaningless to discuss bibliometrics or scientometrics in isolation from a wide variety of other metrics.

As researchers publish more data and computer programs, and establish a constant stream of self-publications through social media, it will seem increasingly archaic to focus on one single type of output. As an ever wider variety of outputs are recognized as an important part of the academic process, librarians are likely to play a more central role in capturing the data. Whereas today evaluative and relational scientometrics focus on calculations based around the citations that can be measured through one of two or three tools, as a greater variety of information avenues are recognized as important it will be necessary for data to be gathered from a greater variety of sources. Whether for assessment purposes, to highlight resources, or merely to map a research environment, researchers are likely to need help to understand the new research environment. They will need to understand the change in types of content that are made available by researchers, and recognize the increasing amounts of work that take place online. This change in the working practices of researchers will enable data scientists to investigate researchers' practices with a finer level of granularity: how are researchers engaging with resources? What can we learn about the working practices of highly cited authors and those who are less well cited? The availability of the data will also raise new questions about how receptive researchers will be to the Taylorization of their working practices, as like the practices of the 19th-century factory worker the researcher's activities are systematically broken down and analysed. As has been shown in behavioural economics, behaviour changes when people know that their work is being watched (Ariely et al., 2009), and it may be that once researchers are aware that their work is being watched, their behaviour changes in unexpected ways. This particular seam of data might not be mined to its full extent for a while yet.

From a practical point of view, there are significant consequences from the rapid pace of change for the development of widely agreed metrics. Journal articles have been published for hundreds of years, yet there is still no agreement about which are the most important metrics for measuring their impact. During a ten year period we can expect a new web service to dominate a community to such an extent that it would be inconceivable not to include journal articles in bibliometric or scientometric investigations, only for them to fall out of favour just as quickly. As a recent editorial on the topic of altmetrics in *Nature Materials* noted: 'any new metrics introduced today may not have time to be validated and gain acceptance' (Nature Materials, 2012, 90). Nonetheless it is important that we do not limit ourselves only to those metrics that have been validated, as we will find that we are quickly outpaced by changes in technology. There is a widespread need for librarians who can engage critically with the development of new metrics, rather than people who merely apply metrics that have been validated by others.

Webometrics

Fundamental changes to the way information is published, disseminated and retrieved over the last two decades have inevitably changed the traditional role of librarians, and will continue to do so as more resources are published online, subscriptions are bundled together, deals are brokered by consortiums, and new online tools are developed that aid in the discovery of content. The information profession is one where as librarians continue to provide traditional library services, they must necessarily look to carve out their niche in the new information environment that makes the best use of their existing skills. The idea that librarians move up the research chain and increasingly work alongside researchers is one that has been gaining an increased amount of interest, and would seem to be an area for growth as e-science and data science are ever more important, and webometrics is necessarily a part of that.

As has already been noted the role of the data scientist draws together three significant skill sets: domain knowledge, computing skills and statistical methods. Librarians are in a strong position to meet those requirements. Domain knowledge is generally considered a requirement of librarians' qualifications, with librarians generally having a degree in a particular specialism as well as a degree in library or information science. 'Hacking skills' refers to the ability to collect and manipulate some of the many information sources that are available. While librarians have little experience of dealing with the large-scale data intensive frameworks (e.g., Hadoop) required for big data analytics, with webometrics much of the processing of big data takes place server-side by external services; for example, when investigating a network of web pages linked by URL citations Bing deals with the problems of collecting and storing a copy of the web while the researcher only has to deal with the handful of pages that is available. Equally important as the 'hacking skills' is the identification of suitable data sources and tools for analysing this data, skills which align closely with those of librarians. Although the statistical methods requirements already play a role in the work of those specializing in bibliometrics, this will not have played a significant role for many within the library profession, but as this book has demonstrated, and as Silver (2012) emphasizes in his work on data science, the statistical methods that need to be applied do not have to be overly complex.

As well as practical skills, librarians also bring a range of other competencies that play an important role in webometric research. Information ethics and intellectual property rights have been a part of the information scientist's work for many years, and are readily placed to deal with the new issues that arise as information that is publicly available is used, aggregated and manipulated in ways that were not originally intended (Oboler, Welsh and Cruz, 2012; Wilkinson and Thelwall, 2011). It is also important to recognize that there is a human element to webometrics: it is necessary to examine the available data sources in the most efficient manner, to ask the right questions and to ensure that people understand the potential of data that is available. Librarians are experienced not only in finding solutions to specific problems, but also in helping users understand what it is they actually want to ask in the form of the reference interview.

Although there is clearly a potential role for librarians in webometrics, or the associated areas of data science and e-science, it is less clear where that post will be based. The role of librarians and the library as a space are undergoing a period of change. It may be that while certain information services are pooled (e.g., data repositories), webometricians and data scientists will work with specific departments as they explore domain knowledge and user requirements.

Taking the first steps

It seems as though web metrics is going to have an increasingly important role for librarians, at least for those in the profession who want it to. This leads to the inevitable question of where librarians should start as there is such a wide variety of metrics that could take place.

When approaching such a complex environment librarians should not get bogged down with the sheer variety of things that could be investigated, but rather start with an easily accessible base from which they can build. Within web metrics this is likely to be web analytics, with librarians' own or their institution's social network presence generally the most appropriate place to start. This book is designed to encourage the exploration of a wide range of the data that is available on the web, rather than just on a library or information service's own web analytics, but it is easy to imagine how the learning curve for certain web metric investigations may be too steep for people to bother with. An investigation into the popularity of ontologies within a particular research area is likely to have far wider interest than a single librarian's Twitter impact, but whereas the ontology investigation may require a wide range of technologies and the development of new methodologies and metrics in this new area of research, the analysis of a Twitter account will be built on the concepts that librarians are aware of. There is the potential for increasingly complicated levels of investigation, for example:

1 Compare the number of followers an account receives with those of similar institutions.
2 Compare the number of followers received by taking into consideration the number of people being followed and the number of status updates by using multiple regression analysis.
3 Carry out a content analysis of recent tweets from one's own account and the most successful accounts to identify potential differences between the types of status updates.

4   Analyse the network created between the Twitter accounts forming the basis of the investigations.
5   Compare the social networks of the friends and followers of two different accounts, e.g., a successful and an unsuccessful account, or accounts that use Twitter in different ways.

Twitter followers may not be a great metric for making comparisons between Twitter accounts, but even this simple metric is likely to be more than librarians have analysed in a methodical manner (as opposed to occasionally comparing their number of followers with those of a friend or colleague in a haphazard manner).

There is little point in calculating metrics for the purpose of web analytics unless they are going to be interpreted and, if necessary, acted on. Whether librarians are going to act on the data they have captured, and undertake a follow-up study a couple of months later, or whether they want to share the findings straight away, librarians need to recognize the importance of using the information to make a case.

As the title for this final section suggests, these are only the first steps. Although a limited number of data and tools are available to web metrics, a greater limitation is the number and type of questions that are asked, and librarians have a lot to offer to overcome this problem.

Bibliography

Acerbi, A., Lampos, V., Garnett, P. and Bentley, R. A. (2013) The Expression of Emotions in 20th Century Books, *PLOS ONE*, **8** (3), e59030.

Achrekar, H., Gandhe, A., Lazarus, R., Ssu-Hsin, Y. and Benyuan, L. (2011) Predicting Flu Trends Using Twitter Data. In *IEEE InfoCom 2011 – IEE Conference on Computer Communications Worshop*, 702–7.

Adamic, L. and Glance, N. (2005) *The Political Blogosphere and the 2004 U.S. Election: divided they blog*, http://nielsen-online.com/downloads/us/buzz/wp_PoliticalBlogosphere_Glance_2004.pdf.

Agger, B. (2012) *Oversharing: presentations of self in the internet age*, Routledge.

Aguillo, I. (1997) *Cybermetrics '97 (Jerusalem, Israel)*, www.cindoc.csic.es/cybermetrics/cybermetrics97.html.

Aguillo, I. (2012) Is Google Scholar Useful for Bibliometrics? A webometric analysis, *Scientometrics*, **91** (3), 343–51.

Aksnes, D. W. and Rip, A. (2009) Researchers' Perceptions of Citations, *Research Policy*, **38** (6), 895–905.

Alexa (2013a) *Frequently Asked Questions: how are Alexa's traffic rankings determined?*, www.alexa.com/faqs/?p=134.

Alexa (2013b) *Site Info: wikipedia.org*, www.alexa.com/siteinfo/wikipedia.org.

Almind, T. C. and Ingwersen, P. (1996) *Informetric Analysis on the World Wide Web: a methodological approach to 'internetometrics'*, Centre for Informetric Studies, Royal School of Library and Information Science (CIS Report 2).

Almind, T. C. and Ingwersen, P. (1997) Informetric Analyses on the World Wide Web: methodological approaches to 'webometrics', *Journal of Documentation*, **53** (4), 404–26.

Anderson, C. (2006) *The Long Tail*, Random House.

Angus, E., Thelwall, M. and Stuart, D. (2008) General Patterns of Tag Usage Among University Groups in Flickr, *Online Information Review*, **32** (1), 89–101.

Ariely, D., Gneezy, U., Loewenstein, G. and Mazar, N. (2009) Large Stakes and Big Mistakes, *Review of Economic Studies*, **76**, 451–69.

Arthur, C. (2013) Google Keep? It'll probably be with us until March 2017 – on average, *Guardian*, www.guardian.co.uk/technology/2013/mar/22/google-keep-services-closed.

Banerjee, A. V. and Duflo, E. (2012) *Poor Economics*, Penguin.

Bar-Ilan, J. (2005) Expectations Versus Reality – search engine features needed for web research at mid 2005, *Cybermetrics*, **9** (paper 2), http://cybermetrics.cindoc.csic.es/articles/v9i1p2.html.

Bar-Ilan, J. (2012) JASIST@mendeley: altmetrics12, *ACM Web Science Conference 2012 Workshop*, http://altmetrics.org/altmetrics12/bar-ilan/.

Bar-Ilan, J. and Azoulay, R. (2013) Map of Non-Profit Organization Websites in Israel, *Journal of the American Society for Information Science and Technology*, **63** (6), 1142–67.

Bar-Ilan, J., Haustein, S., Peters, I., Priem, J., Shema, H. and Terliesner, J. (2012) Beyond Citations: scholars' visibility on the social web, *17th International Conference on Science and Technology Indicators, Montreal, Canada, 5–8 Sept.*

Batke, P. (2010) *Google Books: Google Book Search and its critics*, www.lulu.com/items/volume_68/8362000/8362807/5/print/pbedits.HC.4-26.pdf.

Beckmann, M. and von Wehrden, H. (2012) Where You Search Is What You Get: literature mining – Google Scholar versus Web of Science using a data set from a literature search in vegetation science, *Journal of Vegetation Science*, **23** (6), 1197–9.

Beel, J. and Gipp, B. (2009) Google Scholar's Ranking Algorithm: an introductory overview. In Larsen, B. and Leta, J. (eds), *Proceedings of the 12th International Conference on Scientometrics and Informetrics (ISSI'09)*, Rio de Janeiro, July, International Society for Scientometrics and Informetrics, 230–41.

Beel, J., Gipp, B. and Wilde, E. (2010) *Academic Search Engine Optimization (ASEO): optimizing scholarly literature for Google Scholar and Co.*, www.sciplore.org/publications/2010-ASEO—preprint.pdf.

Behn, R. D. (2003) Why Measure Performance? Different purposes require different measures, *Public Administrative Review*, **63** (5), 586–606.

Benevenuto, F., Duarte, F., Rodrigues, T., Almeida, V., Almedia, J. and Ross, K. (2008) Understanding Video Interactions in YouTube. *MM'08*, October 26–31, Vancouver, British Columbia, Canada.

Bergman, E. M. L. (2012) Finding Citations to Social Work Literature: the relative benefits of using Web of Science, Scopus, or Google Scholar, *Journal of Academic Librarianship*, **38** (6), 370–9.

Berkowitz, D. (2009) *100 Ways to Measure Social Media*, www.marketersstudio.com/2009/11/100-ways-to-measure-social-media-.html.

Berners-Lee, T., Hendler, J. and Lassila, O. (2001) The Semantic Web, *Scientific American*, May, 29–37.

Bertin, M. and Atanassova, I. (2012) Semantic Enrichment of Scientific Publications and Metadata: citation analysis through contextual and cognitive analysis, *D-Lib Magazine*, **18** (7/8), www.dlib.org/dlib/july12/bertin/07bertin.html.

Björneborn, L. and Ingwersen, P. (2004) Toward a Basic Framework for Webometrics, *Journal of the American Society for Information Science and Technology*, **55** (14), 1216–27.

Blood, R. (2000) *Weblogs: a history and perspective, Rebecca's pocket*, www.rebeccablood.net/essays/weblog_history.html.

Bode, K. (2012) *Reading by Numbers: recalibrating the literary field*, Anthem Press.

Borgman, C. L. and Furner, J. (2002) Scholarly Communication and Bibliometrics. In Cronin, B. (ed.), *Annual Review of Information Science and Technology*, **36**, 3–72.

Börner, K., Sanyal, S. and Vespignani, A. (2007) Network Science. In Cronin, B. (ed.), *Annual Review of Information Science & Technology*, **41**, 537–607.

Bornmann, L., Mutz, R. and Daniel, H.-D. (2008) Are There Better Indices for Evaluation Purposes than the *h* Index? A comparison of nine different variants of the *h* index using data from biomedicine, *Journal of the American Society for Information Science and Technology*, **59** (5), 830–7.

Bornoe, N. and Barkhuus, L. (2011) Privacy Management in a Connected World: students' perception of facebook privacy settings, *paper given at Workshop on Collaborative Privacy Practices in Social Media, part of the 2011 ACM Conference on Computer Supported Cooperative Work (CSCW '11), March 19–23, Hangzhou, China*.

Bossy, M. J. (1995) *The Last of the Litter: 'Netometrics', Solaris*, **2**, http://biblio-fr.info.unicaen.fr/bnum/jelec/Solaris/d02/2bossy.html.

Boudourides, M. A., Sigrist, B. and Alevizos, P. D. (1999) *Webometrics and the Self-Organization of the European Information Society*, draft report of the SOEIS project, http://hyperion.math.upatras.gr/webometrics/.

Boyd, D. M. and Ellison, N. B. (2007) Social Network Sites: definition, history, and scholarship, *Journal of Computer-Mediated Communication*, **13** (1), article 11, http://jcmc.indiana.edu/vol13/issue1/boyd.ellison.html.

Brin, S. and Page, L. (1998) The Anatomy of a Large-Scale Hypertextual Web Search Engine, *Computer Networks and ISDN Systems*, **30** (1–7), 107–17.

Broadus, R. N. (1987) Early Approaches to Bibliometrics, *Journal of Information Science*, **38** (2), 127–9.

Broder, A., Kumar, R., Maghoul, F., Raghaven, P., Rajagopalan, S., Stata, R., Tomkin, A. and Wiener, J. (2000) Graph Structure in the Web, *Computer Networks*, **33** (1–6), 309–20.

Bruns, A. and Highfield, T. (2013) Political Networks on Twitter: tweeting the

Queensland state election, *Information Communication & Society*, **16** (5), 667–91.

Butler, D. (2013) When Google got Flu Wrong, *Nature*, **494**, 155–6.

Chan, E. H., Sahai, V., Conrad, C. and Brownstein, J. S. (2011) Using Web Search Query Data to Monitor Dengue Epidemics: a new model for neglected tropical disease surveillance, *PLoS Negl Trop*, **5** (5), e1206.

Chen, C., Newman, J., Newman, R. and Rada, R. (1998) How did University Departments Interweave the Web: a study of connectivity and underlying factors, *Interacting with Computers*, **10** (4), 353–73.

Chew, C. and Eysenbach, G. (2010) Pandemics in the Age of Twitter: content analysis of tweets during the 2009 H1N1 Outbreak, *PLOS ONE*, **5** (11), e14118.

Choi, H. and Varian, H. (2012) Predicting the Present with Google Trends, *Economic Record*, special issue, June, 2–9.

Choi, S., Park, J. Y. and Park, H. W. (2012) Using Social Media Data to Explore Communication Processes Within South Korean Online Communities, *Scientometrics*, **90** (1), 43–56.

Chowdhury, S. A. and Makaroff, D. (2013) Popularity Growth Patterns of YouTube Videos: a category-based study. In Krempels, K. H. and Stocker, A. (eds), *Proceedings of WEBIST 2013: 8th International Conference on Web Information Systems and Technologies*, 233–42.

Christakis, N. and Fowler, J. (2009) *Connected: the amazing power of social networks and how they change lives*, Little, Brown, and Company.

Chung, C. J. and Park, H. W. (2012) Web Visibility of Scholars in Media and Communication Journals, *Scientometrics*, **93** (1), 207–15.

Ciesielski, K., Borkowski, P., Klopotek, M. A., Trojanowski, K. and Wysocki, K. (2012) Wikipedia-based Categorization, Security and Intelligent Information Systems, *Lecture Notes in Computer Science*, vol. 7053, 265–78.

Clauson, K. A., Polen, H. H., Boulos, M. N. K. and Dzenowagis, J. H. (2008) Scope, Completeness, and Accuracy of Drug Information in Wikipedia, *Annals of Pharmacotherapy*, **42**, 1814–21.

Compete (2013) Our Data, www.compete.com/us/about/our-data/.

Cothey, V., Aguillo, I. and Arroyo, N. (2006) Operationalising 'Websites': lexically, semantically or topologically?, *Cybermetrics*, **10** (1), www.cindoc.csic.es/cybermetrics/articles/v10i1p3.html.

Cronin, B. (1984) *The Citation Process*, Taylor Graham.

Cunningham, J. A. (2012) Using Twitter to Measure Behaviour Patterns, *Epidemiology*, **23** (5), 764–5.

Davenport, T. H. and Patil, D. J. (2012) Data Scientist: the sexiest job of the 21st century, *Harvard Business Review*, October.

De Bellis, N. (2009) *Bibliometrics and Citation Analysis: from the Science Citation Index to*

Cybermetrics, Scarecrow Press.

Del Bosque, D., Leif, S. A. and Skarl, S. (2012) Libraries Atwitter: trends in academic library tweeting, *Reference Services Review*, **40** (2), 199–213.

Didegah, F. and Erfanmanesh, M. A. (2010) The Study of Malaysian Public Universities' Performance on the World Wide Web, *Library Hi Tech News*, **27** (3), 7–11.

Dijkstra, E. W. (1968) A Case Against the GO TO Statement, *Communications of the ACM*, **11** (3), 147–8.

Du, R. Y. and Kamakura, W. A. (2012) Quantitative Trendspotting, *Journal of Marketing Research*, **49** (4), 514–36.

Dunbar, R. (2011) *How Many Friends Does One Person Need? Dunbar's number and other evolutionary quirks*, Faber & Faber.

Dzielinski, M. (2012) Measuring Economic Uncertainty and its Impact on the Stock Market, *Finance Research Letters*, **9** (3), 167–75.

Ebersbach, A., Glaser, M. and Heigl, R. (2008) *Wiki: web collaboration*, 2nd edn, Springer.

Edelman, B. and Larkin, I. (2009) *Demographics, Career Concerns or Social Comparison: who games SSRN download counts?*, Harvard Business School NOM Unit Working Paper No. 09-096, www.hbs.edu/research/pdf/09-096.pdf.

Egnal, M. (2013) Evolution of the Novel in the United States: the statistical evidence, *Social Science History*, **37** (2), 231–54.

Ennew, C., Lockett, A., Blackman, I. and Holland, C. P. (2005) Competition in Internet Retail Markets: the impact of links on web site traffic, *Long Range Planning*, **38** (4), 359–72.

Ettredge, M., Gerdes, J. and Karuga, G. (2005) Using Web-Based Search Data to Predict Macroeconomic Statistics, *Communications of the ACM*, **48** (11), 87–92.

Etzkowitz, H. and Leydesdorff, L. (1995) The Triple Helix: university-industry-government relations, *EASST Review*, **14** (1), www.easst.net/review/march1995/leydesdorff.

Eysenbach, G. (2006) Infodemiology: tracking flu-related searches on the web for syndromic surveillance, *American Medical Informatics Association Annual Symposium Proceedings*, 244–8, www.ncbi.nlm.nih.gov/pmc/articles/PMC1839505/.

Eysenbach, G. (2011) Can Tweets Predict Citations? Metrics of social impact based on Twitter and correlations with traditional metrics of scientific impact, *Journal of Medical Internet Research*, **13** (4), e123, www.jmir.org/2011/4/e123/.

Facebook (2012) Newsroom – key facts, http://newsroom.fb.com/Key-Facts.

Feldman, R. (2013) Techniques and Applications for Sentiment Analysis, *Communications of the ACM*, **56** (4), 82–9.

Fields, E. (2010) A Unique Twitter Use for Reference Services, *Library Hi Tech News*,

27 (6), 14–15.

Garfield, E. (1983) *Citation Indexing – its theory and application in science, technology, and humanities*, ISI Press.

Garfield, E. (2006) The History and Meaning of the Journal Impact Factor, *JAMA*, **295** (1), 90–3.

Gibbons, M., Limoges, C., Nowotny, H., Schwartzman, S., Scott, P. and Trow, M. (1994) *The New Production of Knowledge: the dynamics of science and research in contemporary societies*, Sage Publications.

Giles, J. (2005) Internet Encyclopaedias Go Head to Head, *Nature*, **438**, 900–1.

Giles, J. (2012) Making the Links, *Nature*, **448**, 448–50.

Ginsberg, J., Mohebbi, M. H., Patel, R. S., Brammer, M. S., Smolinski and Brilliant, L. (2009) Detecting Influenza Epidemics Using Search Engine Query Data, *Nature*, **457**, 1012–14.

Glynn, R. W., Kelly, J. C., Coffey, N., Sweeney, K. J. and Kerin, M. J. (2011) The Effect of Breast Cancer Awareness Month on Internet Search Activity – a comparison with awareness campaigns for lung and prostate cancer, *BMC Cancer*, **11**, article 442.

Go, A., Bhayani, R. and Huang, L. (2009) *Twitter Sentiment Classification Using Distant Supervision*, technical report, Stanford, http://cs.stanford.edu/people/alecmgo/papers/TwitterDistantSupervision09.pdf.

Godin, B. (2006) On the Origins of Bibliometrics, *Scientometrics*, **68** (1), 109–33.

Golder, S. A. and Macy, M. W. (2011) Diurnal and Seasonal Mood Vary with Work, Sleep, and Daylength Across Diverse Cultures, *Science*, **333**, 30 September, 1878–81.

Google (2013) Google: Webmaster Tools – what file types can Google Index?, http://support.google.com/webmasters/bin/answer.py?hl=en&answer=35287.

Granovetter, M. S. (1973) The Strength of Weak Ties, *American Journal of Sociology*, **78** (6), 1360–80.

Gruber, T. R. (1993) A Translation Approach to Portable Ontology Specifications, *Knowledge Acquisitions*, **5** (2), 199–220.

Guardian (2012) University Guide 2013: university league table, *Guardian*, 21 May, www.guardian.co.uk/education/table/2012/may/21/university-league-table-2013.

Halpern, D. and Gibbs, J. (2013) Social Media as a Catalyst for Online Deliberation? Exploring the affordances of Facebook and YouTube for political expression, *Computers in Human Behaviour*, **29** (3), 1159–68.

Hand, C. and Judge, G. (2012) Searching for the Picture: forecasting UK cinema admissions using Google Trends data, *Applied Economics Letters*, **19** (11), 1051–5.

Hardiman, S. J. and Katzir, L. (2013) Estimating Clustering Coefficients and Size of Social Networks Via Random Walk, *WWW2013, May 13–17, Rio de Janeiro, Brazil*.

Hardy, Q. (2012) Harvard Releases Big Data For Books, *New York Times: Bits*,
    http://bits.blogs.nytimes.com/2012/04/24/harvard-releases-big-data-for-books.

Harnad, S., Carr, L., Brody, T. and Oppenheim, C. (2003) Mandated Online RAE CVs
    Linked to University Eprint Archives: enhancing UK research impact and
    assessment, *Ariadne*, **35**, www.ariadne.ac.uk/issue35/harnad.

Harter, S. P. and Ford, C. E. (2000) Web-based Analyses of E-Journal Impact:
    approaches, problems, and issues, *Journal of the American Society for Information
    Science*, **51** (13), 1159–76.

He, W., Chee, T., Chong, D. and Rasnick, E. (2012) Using Bibliometrics and Text
    Mining to Explore the Trends of E-Marketing Literature from 2001 to 2010,
    International Journal of Online Marketing, **2** (1), 16–24.

Himelboim, I., McCreery, S. and Smith, M. (2013) Birds of a Feather Tweet Together:
    integrating network and content analysis to examine cross-ideology exposure on
    Twitter, *Journal of Computer-Mediated Communication*, **18** (2), 40–60.

Hirsch, J. E. (2005) An Index to Quantify an Individual's Scientific Research Output,
    Proceedings of the National Academy of Sciences of the United States of America,
    102 (46), 16569–72.

Holmberg, K. (2009) *Webometric Network Analysis – mapping cooperation and
    geopolitical connections between local government administration on the Web*,
    dissertation, Åbo: Åbo Akademi UP.

Hood, W. W. and Wilson, C. S. (2001) The Literature of Bibliometrics, Scientometrics,
    and Informetrics, *Scientometrics*, **52**, 291–314.

Hrynaszkiewicz, I. (2013) Version Control for Scientific Research, *BioMed Central
    blog*, http://blogs.biomedcentral.com/bmcblog/2013/02/28/version-control-for-
    scientific-research.

Hsu, C. L. and Park, H. W. (2012a) Korean and Chinese Webpage Content: who are
    talking about what and how?, *Journal of Computer-Mediated Communication*, **17** (2),
    202–15.

Hsu, C. L. and Park, H. W. (2012b) Mapping Online Social Networks of Korean
    Politicians, *Government Information Quarterly*, **29** (2), 169–81.

Hubbard, D. W. (2011) *Pulse*, John Wiley & Sons.

Hung, J. (2012) Trends of E-Learning Research from 2000–2008: use of text mining
    and bibliometrics, *British Journal of Educational Technology*, **43** (1), 5–16.

Information Commission Office (2012) *The EU Cookie Law*,
    www.ico.gov.uk/for_organisations/privacy_and_electronic_communications/
    the_guide/cookies.aspx.

Ingwersen, P. (1998) The Calculation of Web Impact Factors, *Journal of
    Documentation*, **54** (2), 236–43.

Internet Archive (2012) 80 Terabytes of Archived Web Crawl Data Available for

Research: internet archive blogs, http://blog.archive.org/2012/10/26/80-terabytes-of-archived-web-crawl-data-available-for-research.

Jackson, J. (2010) *Google: 129 million different books have been published*, www.pcworld.com/article/202803/google_129_million_different_books_have_been_published.html.

Jacso, P. (2012) Google Scholar Metrics for Publications: the software and content features of a new open access bibliometric service, *Online Information Review*, **36** (4), 604–19.

Journalism.org (2005) *Seigenthaler and Wikipedia: a case study on the veracity of the 'wiki' concept*, www.journalism.org/node/1672.

Kaplan, A. M. and Haenlein, M. (2010) Users of the World, Unite! The challenges and opportunities of social media, *Business Horizons*, **53**, 59–68.

Kazienko, P., Szozda, N., Filipowski, T. and Blysz, W. (2013) New Business Client Acquisition Using Social Networking Sites, *Electronic Markets*, **23** (2), 93–103.

Kepler, T. B., Marti-Renom, M. A., Maurer, S. M., Rai, A. K., Taylor, G. and Todd, M. H. (2006) Open Source Research – the power of us, *Australian Journal of Chemistry*, **59** (5), 291–4.

Kim, H. M., Abels, E. G. and Yang, C. C. (2012) Who Disseminates Academic Library Information on Twitter, *Proceedings of the American Society for Information Science and Technology*, **49** (1), 1–4.

Kimmons, R. (2011) Understanding Collaboration in Wikipedia, *First Monday*, **16** (12), http://firstmonday.org/ojs/index.php/fm/article/view/3613/3117.

Kousha, K. and Thelwall, M. (2006) Motivations for URL Citations to Open Access Library and Information Science Articles, *Scientometrics*, **68** (3), 501–17.

Kousha, K. and Thelwall, M. (2008) Assessing the Impact of Disciplinary Research on Teaching: an automatic analysis of online syllabuses, *Journal of the American Society for Information Science and Technology*, **59** (13), 2060–9.

Kousha, K., Thelwall, M. and Rezaie, S. (2011) Assessing the Citation Impact of Books: the role of Google Books, Google Scholar, and Scopus, *Journal of the American Society for Information Science and Technology*, **62** (11), 2147–64.

Krauth, S. J., Coulibaly, J. T., Knopp, S., Traoré, M., N'Goran, E. K. and Utzinger, J. (2012) An In-Depth Analysis of a Piece of Shit: distribution of Schistosoma mansoni and hookworm eggs in human stool, *PLoS Neglected Tropical Diseases*, **6** (12), e1969.

Krippendorff, K. H. (2012) *Content Analysis: an introduction to its methodology*, 3rd edn, Sage Publications.

Kronick, D. A. (1990) Peer Review in 18th-century Scientific Journalism, *Journal of the American Medical Association*, **263** (10), 1321–2.

Kuper, S. and Szymanski, S. (2012) *Soccernomics*, HarperSport.

Kwan, Y. and Chan, L. M. (2009) Linking Folksonomy to Library of Congress Subject Headings: an exploratory study, *Journal of Documentation*, **65** (5), 872–900.

Lai, K. F. and Wang, D. (2013) Understanding the External Links of Video Sharing Sites: measurement and analysis, *IEEE Transactions on Multimedia*, **15** (1), 224–35.

Larson, R. R. (1996) Bibliometrics of the World Wide Web: an exploratory analysis of the intellectual structure of cyber space. In Hardin, S. (ed.), *Proceedings of the 59th Annual Meeting, ASIS*, Learned Information Ltd, 71–9.

Lawrence, P. A. (2007) Popular Beat May Drown Out Genius, *Times Higher Education*, 24 August, www.timeshighereducation.co.uk/310247.article.

Lazarev, V. S. (1996) On Chaos in Bibliometric Terminology, *Scientometrics*, **35** (2), 271–7.

Lewis, M. (2004) *Moneyball*, W. W. Norton.

Li, L. (2011) Social Network Site Comparison Between the United States and China: case study on Facebook and Renren network. In *Proceedings of the 2011 International Conference on Business Management and Electronic Information*, 825–7.

Li, X., Thelwall, M., Musgrove, P. and Wilkinson, D. (2003) The Relationship Between the WIFs or Inlinks of Computer Science Departments in the UK and their RAE Ratings or Research Productivities in 2001, *Scientometrics*, **57** (2), 239–55.

Lipsett, A. (2006) Metrics Will Kill Diversity Claim, *Times Higher Education*, 15 December, www.timeshighereducation.co.uk/news/metrics-will-kill-diversity-claim/207149.article.

Lipsett, A. (2007) Report: bibliometrics could distort research assessment, *Guardian*, 9 November, www.theguardian.com/education/2007/nov/09/highereducation. researchassessmentexercise.

Liu, B. (2012) *Sentiment Analysis and Opinion Mining*, Morgan & Claypool Publishers.

Lowry, O. H., Rosebrough, N. J., Farr, A. L. and Randall, R. J. (1951) Protein Measurement with the Folin Phenol Reagent, *Journal of Biological Chemistry*, **193** (1), 265–75.

Lundvall, B. A. (ed.) (1992) *National Systems of Innovation: towards a theory of innovation and interactive learning*, Pinter.

MacRoberts, M. H. and MacRoberts, B. R. (1996) Problems of Citation Analysis, *Scientometrics*, **36** (3), 435–44.

Madden, K., Nan, X., Briones, R. and Waks, L. (2012) A Content Analysis of HPV Vaccine Information Online, *Vaccine*, **30** (25), 3741–6.

Marek, K. (2011) Using Web Analytics in the Library, *Library Technology Reports*, **47** (5).

Marriner, N. and Morhange, C. (2013) Data Mining the Intellectual Revival of 'Catastrophic' Mother Nature, *Foundations of Science*, **18** (2), 245–57.

Mendeley (2012) *Global Research Report*, www.mendeley.com/global-research-report.

Microformats (2012) Microformats at 7,
http://microformats.org/2012/06/25/microformats-org-at-7.

Microsoft (2012) Microsoft Academic Search API,
http://academic.research.microsoft.com/about/Microsoft%20Academic%20
Search%20API%20User%20Manual.pdf.

Milstein, S. (2009) Twitter for Libraries and Librarians, *Computers in Libraries*, **29** (5),
17–18.

Minguillo, D. and Thelwall, M. (2012) Mapping the Network Structure of Science
Parks: an exploratory study of cross-sectoral interactions reflected on the web,
Aslib Proceedings, **64** (4), 332–57.

Moed, H. (2005) *Citation Analysis in Research Evaluation*, Springer.

Mola-Velasco, S. M. and Rosso, P. (2011) Wikipedia Vandalism Detection. In
Proceedings of the 20th International Conference Companion on World Wide Web
(WWW), 391–6.

Mortensen, P. S. (2011) *Patentometrics as Performance Indicators for Allocating Funding
to Universities*, http://pure.au.dk/portal/files/39714215/WP2011_1_Patentometrics_
as_performance_indicators.pdf.

Mukewar, S., Mani, P., Wu, X. R., Lopez, R. and Shen, B. (2013) YouTube and
Inflammatory Bowel Disease, *Journal of Crohns & Colitis*, **7** (5), 392–402.

Narin, F. (1994) Patent Bibliometrics, *Scientometrics*, **30** (1), 147–55.

Nature Materials (2012) Alternative Metrics: editorial, *Nature Materials*, **11**, 907,
www.nature.com/nmat/journal/v11/n11/full/nmat3485.html.

Noyons, E. (2001) Bibliometric Analysis of Science in a Science Policy Context,
Scientometrics, **50** (1), 83–98.

Oboler, A., Welsh, K. and Cruz, L. (2012) The Danger of Big Data: social media as
computational social science, *First Monday*, **17** (7), http://firstmonday.org/
htbin/cgiwrap/bin/ojs/index.php/fm/article/view/3993/3269.

OED (2001) *Metric*, Oxford English Dictionary, www.oed.com/view/Entry/117657.

Orduña-Malea, E. and Ontalba-Ruiperez, J. A. (2013) Selective Linking from Social
Platforms to University Websites: a case study of the Spanish academic system,
Scientometrics, **95** (2), 593–614.

Orduña-Malea, E. and Regazzi, J. J. (2013) US Academic Libraries: understanding
their web presence and their relationship with economic indicators,
Scientometrics, http://link.springer.com/article/10.1007%2Fs11192-013-1001-0.

O'Reilly, T. (2005) *What is Web 2.0: design patterns and business models for the next
generation of software*, http://oreilly.com/pub/a/web2/archive/what-is-web-20.html.

Ortega, J. L. and Aguillo, I. F. (2008) Visualization of the Nordic Academic Web: link
analysis using social network tools, *Information Processing & Management*, **44** (4),

1624–33.

Ortega, J. L. and Aguillo, I. F. (2012) Science is All in the Eye of the Beholder: keyword maps in Google Scholar citations, *Journal of the American Society for Information Science and Technology*, **62** (12), 2370–7.

Ortega, J. L. and Aguillo, I.F. (2013) Institutional and Country Collaboration in an Online Service of Scientific Profiles: Google Scholar citations, *Journal of Informetrics*, **7** (2), 394–403.

Ortiz, J. R., Zhou, H., Shay, D. K., Neuzil, K. M. and Goss, C. H. (2010) Does Google Influenza Tracking Correlate with Laboratory Tests Positive for Influenza?, *American Journal of Respiratory Critical Care Medicine*, **181**, A2626.

Otte, E. and Rousseau, R. (2002) Social Network Analysis: a powerful strategy, also for the information sciences, *Journal of Information Sciences*, **28** (6), 441–53.

Oyelude, A. A. and Bamigbola, A. A. (2012) Libraries as the Gate: 'ways' and 'keepers' in the knowledge environment, *Library Hi Tech News*, **29** (8), 7–10.

Ozel, B. and Park, H. W. (2012) Online Image Content Analysis of Political Figures: an exploratory study, *Quality and Quantity*, **46** (4), 1013–24.

Paltoglou, G., Thelwall M. and Buckley K. (2010) Online Textual Communications Annotated with Grades of Emotion Strength. In *Proceedings of the 3rd International Workshop of Emotion: corpora for research on Emotion and Affect*, 25–31.

Pantelidis, I. S. (2010) Electronic Meal Experience: a content analysis of online restaurant comments, *Cornell Hospitality Quarterly*, **51** (4), 483–91.

Park, H. W., Barnett, G. A. and Nam, I.-Y. (2002) Hyperlink-Affiliation Network Structure of Top Web Sites: examining affiliates with hyperlink in Korea, *Journal of the American Society for Information Science and Technology*, **53** (7), 592–601.

Paul, J. A., Baker, H. M. and Cochran, J. D. (2012) Effect of Online Social Networking on Student Academic Performance, *Computers in Human Behaviour*, **28** (6), 2117–27.

Pesch, O. (2007) Usage Statistics, *Information Service & Use*, **207**, 207–13.

Piwowar, H. (2013) Value All Research Products, *Nature*, **493**, 159.

Piwowar, H. A., Carlson, J. D. and Vision, T. J. (2011) Beginning to Track 1000 Datasets from Public Repositories into the Published Literature, *Proceedings of the American Society for Information Science and Technology*, **48** (1), 1–4.

Polanyi, M. (1966) *The Tacit Dimension*, University of Chicago Press.

Ponce, B. A., Determann, J. R., Boohaker, H. A., Sheppard, E., McGwin, G. and Theiss, S. (2013) Social Networking Profiles and Professionalism Issues in Residency Applicants: an original study-cohort study, *Journal of Surgical Education*, **70** (4), 502–7.

Popegrutch (2011) *Marketing Academic Libraries Through Social Media: resources and examples*, http://popegrutch.wordpress.com/2011/02/23/marketing-academic-libraries-through-social-media-resources-examples.

Price, A. and Grann, V. R. (2012) Portrayal of Complementary and Alternative Medicine for Cancer by Top Online News Sites, *Journal of Alternative and Complementary Medicine*, **18** (5), 487–93.

Price, D. J. S. (1963) *Little Science, Big Science*, Columbia University Press.

Priem, J., Taraborelli, D., Groth, P. and Neylon, C. (2010) *Altmetrics: a manifesto*, http://altmetrics.org/manifesto.

Pries, T., Moat, H. S., Stanley, H. E. and Bishop, S. R. (2012) Quantifying the Advantage of Looking Forward, *Scientific Reports*, www.ncbi.nlm.nih.gov/pmc/articles/PMC3320057.

Pritchard, A. (1969) Statistical Bibliography or Bibliometrics?, *Journal of Documentation*, **25** (4), 348–9.

Quantcast (2013) How We Do It, www.quantcast.com/how-we-do-it/methodology.

Quint, B. (1998) A 'Gift of the Web' for the Library of Congress from Alexa Internet, *Information Today*,

http://newsbreaks.infotoday.com/nbreader.asp?ArticleID=17893.

Ranganathan, S. R. (1931) *Five Laws of Library Science*, Madras Library Association.

Raymond, E. S. (2001) *The Cathedral and the Bazaar: musings on the Linux and Open Source by an accidental revolutionary*, O'Reilly Media.

Rector, L. H. (2008) Comparison of Wikipedia and Other Encyclopedias for Accuracy, Breadth, and Depth in Historical Articles, *Reference Services Review*, **36** (1), 7–22.

Rolnick, A. J. and Weber, W. E. (1986) Gresham's Law or Gresham's Fallacy, *Journal of Political Economy*, **94** (1), 185–99.

Rorick, W. C. (1987) Discometrics – a system for acquiring scores and sound recordings, *Library Journal*, **112** (19), 45–7.

Rousseau, R. (1997) Sitations: an exploratory study, *Cybermetrics*, **1** (1), http://cybermetrics.cindoc.csic.es/pruebas/v1i1p1.htm.

Russell, A. L. (2005) Standardization in History: a review essay with an eye to the future. In Bolin, S. (ed.), *The Standards Edge: future generations*, Sheridan Press, 247–60.

Schreiber, M., Malesios, C. C. and Psarakis, S. (2012) Exploratory Factor Analysis for the Hirsch Index, 17 h-type variants and some traditional bibliometric indicators, *Journal of Informetrics*, **6** (3), 347–58.

Schubert, A. (2012) Jazz Discometrics – a network approach, *Journal of Informetrics*, **6** (4), 480–4.

Schuster, N. M., Rogers, M. A. M. and McMahon, L. F. (2010) Using Search Engine Query Data to Track Pharmaceutical Utilization: a study of statins, *American Journal of Managed Care*, **16** (8), E215–19.

Seifter, A., Schwarzwalder, A., Geis, K. and Aucott, J. (2010) The Utility of 'Google Trends' for Epidemiological Research: Lyme disease as an example, *Geospatial Health*, **4** (2), 135–7.

Sewell, R. R. (2013) Who Is Following Us? Data mining a library's Twitter followers, *Library Hi Tech*, **31** (1), 160–70.

Shapiro, F. R. (1992) Origins of Bibliometrics, Citation Indexing, and Citation Analysis: the neglected legal literature, *Journal of the American Society for Information Science*, **43** (5), 337–9.

Shuai, X., Pepe, A. and Bollen, J. (2012) How the Scientific Community Reacts to Newly Submitted Preprints: article downloads, Twitter mentions, and citations, *PLOS ONE*, **7** (11), e47523.

Silver, N. (2012) *The Signal and the Noise: the art and science of prediction*, Allen Lane.

Simpson, C. (2008) Five Laws, *Library Media Connection*, April/May, 6.

Singer, R. (2009) Content Sources and Mashing Them Up. In Engard, N. (ed.), *Library Mashups: exploring new ways to deliver library data*, Facet Publishing.

Skolnik, H. (1979) Historical Development of Abstracting, *Journal of Chemical Information and Computer Science*, **19** (4), 215–18.

Smith, A. (1999) *ANZAC Webometrics: exploring Australasian web structures*, http://conferences.alia.org.au/online1999/proceedings99/203b.html.

Sterne, J. (2010) *Social Media Metrics*, John Wiley & Sons.

Stonier, T. (1999) Information as a Basic Property of the Universe, *Biosystems*, **38** (2–3), 135–40.

Strathern, M. (1997) 'Improving Ratings': audit in the British University system, *European Review*, **5** (3), 305–21.

Strychowsky, J. E., Nayan, S., Farrokhyar, F., Maclean, J. (2013) YouTube: a good source of information on pediatric tonsillectomy?, *International Journal of Pediatric Otorhinolaryngology*, **77** (6), 972–5.

Stuart, D. (2010) What Are Libraries Doing on Twitter?, *Online*, **34** (1), 45–7.

Stuart, D. (2011) *Facilitating Access to the Web of Data: a guide for librarians*, Facet Publishing.

Stuart, D. (2012) FOAF Within UK Academic Web Space: a webometric analysis of the semantic web. In Widén, G. and Holmberg, K. (eds), *Social Information Research*, Emerald Publishing, 173–91.

Stuart, D. and Thelwall, M. (2006) Investigating Triple Helix Relationships Using URL Citations: a case study of the UK West Midlands automobile industry, *Research Evaluation*, **15** (2), 97–106.

Stuart, D. and Thelwall, M. (2007) University-Industry-Government Relationships Manifested Through MSN Reciprocal Links. In Torres-Salinas, D. and Moed, H. F. (eds), *Proceedings of the 11th International Conference of the International Society for*

Scientometrics and Informetrics, vol. 2, Madrid: CINDOC, 731–5.

Stuart, D., Thelwall, M. and Harries, G. (2007) UK Academic Web Links and Collaboration – an exploratory study, *Journal of Information Science*, **33** (2), 231–46.

Sueki, H. (2011) Does the Volume of Internet Searches Using Suicide-Related Search Terms Influence the Suicide Death Rate: data from 2004 to 2009 in Japan, *Psychiatry and Clinical Neurosciences*, **65** (4), 392–4.

Sugimoto, C. R., Thelwall, M., Lariviere, V., Tsou, A., Mongeon, P. and Macaluso, B. (2013) Scientists Popularising Science: characteristics and impact of TED talk, *PLOS ONE*, **8** (4), e62403.

Sullivan, D. (2012) *Google: 100 billion searches per month, search to integrate Gmail, launching enhanced search app for iOS*, http://searchengineland.com/google-search-press-129925.

Sullivan, D. (2013) *Marketing Land: Chrome to gain search encryption, following similar moves by Firefox & Mobile Safari*, http://marketingland.com/chrome-to-gain-encryption-31085.

Swanson, D. R. (1986) Fish Oil, Raynaud's Syndrome, and Undiscovered Public Knowledge, *Perspectives in Biology and Medicine*, **30** (1), 7–18.

Tague-Sutcliffe, J. (1992) An Introduction to Informetrics, *Information Processing & Management*, **38** (1), 1–3.

Tancer, B. (2009) *Click: what we do online and why it matters*, Harper Collins.

Thelwall, M. (2001a) Exploring the Link Structure of the Web with Network Diagrams, *Journal of Information Science*, **27** (6), 393–401.

Thelwall, M. (2001b) Results from a Web Impact Factor Crawler, *Journal of Documentation*, **57** (2), 177–91.

Thelwall, M. (2002) Conceptualizing the Documentation on the Web: an evaluation of different heuristic-based models for counting links between university web sites, *Journal of the American Society for Information Science and Technology*, **53** (12), 995–1005.

Thelwall, M. (2004a) *Link Analysis: an information science approach*, Elsevier Academic Press.

Thelwall, M. (2004b) Weak Benchmarking Indicators for Formative and Semi-Evaluative Assessment of Research, *Research Evaluation*, **13** (1), 63–8.

Thelwall, M. (2008) Social Networks, Gender, and Friending: an analysis of MySpace member profiles, *Journal of the American Society for Information Science and Technology*, **59** (8), 1321–30.

Thelwall, M. (2009) *Introduction to Webometrics: quantitative web research for the social sciences*, Morgan & Claypool.

Thelwall, M. (2012) Journal Impact Evaluation: a webometric perspective, *Scientometrics*, **92** (2), 429–41.

Thelwall, M. and Price, L. (2003) Disciplinary Differences in Academic Web
    Presence: a statistical study of the UK, *Libri*, **53** (4), 242–53.
Thelwall, M. and Stuart, D. (2006) Web Crawling Ethics Revisited: cost, privacy, and
    denial of service, *Journal of the American Society of Information Science and
    Technology*, **57** (13), 1771–9.
Thelwall, M. and Stuart, D. (2010) Social Network Sites: an exploration of features
    and diversity. In Zaphiris, P. and Ang, C. S. (eds), *Social Computing and Virtual
    Communities*, CRC, 265–84.
Thelwall, M. and Sud, P. (2011) A Comparison of Methods for Collecting Web
    Citation Data for Academic Organizations, *Journal of the American Society for
    Information Science and Technology*, **62** (8), 1488–97.
Thelwall, M. and Sud, P. (2012) Webometric Research with Bing Search API 2.0,
    Journal of Informetrics, **6** (1), 44–52.
Thelwall, M. and Wilkinson, D. (2004) Finding Similar Academic Web Sites with
    Links, Bibliometric Couplings and Colinks, *Information Processing & Management*,
    40 (3), 515–26.
Thelwall, M., Harries, G. and Wilkinson, D. (2003) Why do Web Sites from Different
    Academic Subjects Interlink?, *Journal of Information Science*, **29** (6), 453–71.
Thelwall, M., Haustein, S., Larivière, V. and Sugimoto, C. R. (2013) Do Altmetrics
    Work? Twitter and ten other social web services, *PLOS ONE*, **8** (5): e64841.
Thornton, E. (2012) Is Your Academic Library Pinning? Academic libraries and
    Pinterest, *Journal of Web Librarianship*, **6** (3), 164–75.
Torres-Salinas, D., Cabezas-Clavijo, A. and Ruiz-Perez, R. (2011) State of the Library
    and Information Science Blogosphere After Social Networks Boom: a metric
    approach, *Library & Information Science Research*, **33** (2), 168–74.
Turow, J. (2011) *The Daily You: how the advertising industry is defining your identity and
    worth*, Yale University Press.
Twenge, J. M., Campbell, W. K. and Gentile, B. (2012a) Increases in Individualistic
    Words and Phrases in American Books, 1960–2008, *PLOS ONE*, **7** (7), e40181.
Twenge, J. M., Campbell, W. K. and Gentile, B. (2012b) Male and Female Pronoun
    Use in US Books Reflects Women's Status, 1900–2008, *Sex Roles*, **67** (9–10), 488–93.
Twitter (2013) Celebrating #Twitter7,
    https://blog.twitter.com/2013/celebrating-twitter7.
UNESCO (1985) *Recommendation Concerning the International Standardization of
    Statistics Relating to Book Production and Periodicals*,
    http://portal.unesco.org/en/ev.php-
    URL_ID=13068&URL_DO=DO_TOPIC&URL_SECTION=201.html.
US Postal Service (2012) *Books: general: definition of a book*,
    http://pe.usps.com/text/pub2/pub2c6_002.html.

Van Noorden, R. (2012) What Were the Top Papers of 2012 on Social Media?, *Nature News Blog*, http://blogs.nature.com/news/2012/12/what-were-the-top-papers-of-2012-on-social-media.html.

Van Noorden, R. (2013) Tensions Grow as Data-Mining Discussions Fall Apart, *Nature*, **498**, 14–15.

Vaughan, L. (2006) Visualizing Linguistic and Cultural Differences Using Web Co-Link Data, *Journal of the American Society for Information Science and Technology*, **57** (9), 1178–93.

Vaughan, L. (2012) An Alternative Data Source for Web Hyperlink Analysis: 'Sites Linking In' at Alexa Internet, *COLLNET Journal of Scientometrics and Information Management*, **6** (4), 31–42.

Vaughan, L. and Romero-Frías, E. (2012) Exploring Web Keyword Analysis as an Alternative to Link Analysis: a multi-industry case, *Scientometrics*, **93** (1), 217–32.

Vaughan, L. and Yang, R. (2012) Web Data as Academic and Business Quality Estimates: a comparison of three data sources, *Journal of the American Society for Information Science and Technology*, **63** (10), 1960–72.

Vaughan, L., Gao, Y. and Kipp, M. (2006) Why are Hyperlinks to Business Websites Created? A content analysis, *Scientometrics*, **67** (2), 291–300.

Vera, C. R. T. (2009) Open Notebook Science: an exploratory study on motivations and perceived challenges. In Shuhua, H. and Thota, H. (eds), *Proceedings of the 4th International Conference on Product Information Management*, 1779–85.

Vosen, S. and Schmidt, T. (2012) A Monthly Consumption Indicator for Germany Based on Internet Search Query, *Applied Economics Letters*, **19** (7), 683–7.

Voß, J. (2005) Measuring Wikipedia. In P. Ingwersen and B. Larsen (eds), *Proceedings of the 10th International Conference of the International Society for Scientometrics and Informetrics*, vol. 1, Stockholm: Karolinska University Press, 221–31.

Vucovich, L. E., Gordon, V. S., Mitchell, N. and Ennis, L. A. (2013) Is the Time and Effort Worth It? One library's evaluation of using social networking tools for outreach, *Medical Reference Services Quarterly*, **32** (1), 12–25.

W3C (2012a) Ontology Dowsing, www.w3.org/wiki/Ontology_Dowsing.

W3C (2012b) RDFa 1.1 Primer, www.w3.org/TR/2012/NOTE-rdfa-primer-20120607/#html-vs.-xhtml.

W3Techs (2013) Usage Statistics and Market Share of Google Analytics for websites, http://w3techs.com/technologies/details/ta-googleanalytics/all/all.

Wagstaff, A. and Culyer, A. J. (2012) Four Decades of Health Economics Through a Bibliometric Lens, *Journal of Health Economics*, **31** (2), 406–39.

Walcott, B. P., Nahed, B. V., Kahle, K. T., Redjal, N. and Coumans, J. V. (2011) Determination of Geographic Variance in Stroke Prevalence Using Internet Search Engine Analytics, *Neurosurgical Focus*, **30** (6), E19.

White, H. D. and McCain, K. W. (1989) Bibliometrics. In Williams, M. E. (ed.), *Annual Review of Information Science and Technology*, **24**, 119–86.

White, H. D., Boell, S. K., Yu, H., Davis, M., Wilson, S. and Cole, F. T. H. (2009) Libcitations: a measure for comparative assessment of book publications in the humanities and social sciences, *Journal of the American Society for Information Science and Technology*, **60** (6), 1083–96.

Wikimedia Foundation (2011) Editor Survey Report, http://commons.wikimedia.org/wiki/File%3AEditor_Survey_Report_-_April_2011.pdf.

Wikipedia (2013a) List of Social Networking Sites, http://en.wikipedia.org/wiki/List_of_social_networking_websites

Wikipedia (2013b) Wikipedia: Wikipedia Loves Libraries, http://en.wikipedia.org/wiki/Wikipedia:Wikipedia_Loves_Libraries.

Wikipedia (2013c) Wikipedians, http://en.wikipedia.org/wiki/Wikipedia:Wikipedians.

Wilkinson, D. and Huberman, B. (2007) Assessing the Value of Cooperation in Wikipedia, *First Monday*, **12** (4), http://firstmonday.org/ojs/index.php/fm/article/view/1763/1643.

Wilkinson, D. and Thelwall, M. (2011) Researching Personal Information on the Public Web: methods and ethics, *Social Science Computer Review*, **29** (4), 387–401.

Wilkinson, D. and Thelwall, M. (2012) Trending Topics in English: an international comparison, *Journal of the American Society for Information Science and Technology*, **63** (8), 1631–46.

Wong, V. S. S., Stevenson, M. and Selwa, L. (2013) The Presentation of Seizures and Epilepsy in YouTube Videos, *Epilepsy & Behaviour*, **27** (1), 247–50.

Xiang, X. (2012) Linguistic and Cultural Characteristics of Domain Names of the Top Fifty Most-Visited Web Sites in the US and China: a cross-linguistic study of domain names and e-branding, *Names – A Journal of Onomastics*, **60** (4), 210–19.

Yan, E., Ding, Y. and Zhu, Q. (2010) Mapping Library and Information Science in China: a coauthorship network analysis, *Scientometrics*, **83** (1), 115-31.

Yeo, G. (2010) *Introduction to Archives: principles and practices*, Facet Publishing.

Zhan, Y. and Yan, Y. (2011) Construction and Optimization of Recruitment Websites in China. In *Fourth International Conference on Business Intelligence and Financial Engineering (BIFE)*, 143–6.

Zhang, X., Fuehres, H. and Gloor, P. A. (2012) Predicting Asset Value through Twitter Buzz, *Advances in Collective Intelligence 2011*, 23–34.

Zhang, Y., He, D. and Sang, Y. (2013) Facebook as a Platform for Health Information and Communication: a case study of a diabetes group, *Journal of Medical Systems*, **37** (3), article 9942.

Ziman, J. M. (1969) Information, Communication, Knowledge, *Nature*, **224**, 318–24.

Index